D3.js Quick Start Guide

Create amazing, interactive visualizations in the browser
with JavaScript

Matthew Huntington

BIRMINGHAM - MUMBAI

D3.js Quick Start Guide

Commissioning Editor: Kunal Chaudari
Acquisition Editor: Noyonika Das
Content Development Editor: Mohammed Yusuf Imaratwale
Technical Editor: Sushmeeta Jena
Copy Editor: Safis Editing
Project Coordinator: Hardik Bhinde
Proofreader: Safis Editing
Indexer: Rekha Nair
Graphics: Alishon Mendonsa
Production Coordinator: Shantanu Zagade

First published: September 2018

Production reference: 1260918

Published by Packt Publishing Ltd.
Livery Place
35 Livery Street
Birmingham
B3 2PB, UK.

ISBN 978-1-78934-238-3

www.packtpub.com

`mapt.io`

Mapt is an online digital library that gives you full access to over 5,000 books and videos, as well as industry leading tools to help you plan your personal development and advance your career. For more information, please visit our website.

Why subscribe?

- Spend less time learning and more time coding with practical eBooks and Videos from over 4,000 industry professionals

- Improve your learning with Skill Plans built especially for you

- Get a free eBook or video every month

- Mapt is fully searchable

- Copy and paste, print, and bookmark content

Packt.com

Did you know that Packt offers eBook versions of every book published, with PDF and ePub files available? You can upgrade to the eBook version at `www.packt.com` and as a print book customer, you are entitled to a discount on the eBook copy. Get in touch with us at `customercare@packtpub.com` for more details.

At `www.packt.com`, you can also read a collection of free technical articles, sign up for a range of free newsletters, and receive exclusive discounts and offers on Packt books and eBooks.

Contributors

About the author

Matthew Huntington has worked as a developer for about 15 years now, and has a full understanding of all aspects of development (server side, client side, and mobile). He graduated magna cum laude from Vassar College with a degree in computer science in which he received departmental honors. He's worked for many clients in New York, including Nike, IBM, Pfizer, MTV, Chanel, Verizon, Goldman Sachs, Nestle, AARP, and BAM. He's worked with companies in pretty much all of the major industries applicable to development, and he has a deep understanding of the differences in the ways those industries work.

As an instructor, Matt has been teaching full-time since 2015 at General Assembly and has lead workshops at many locations, including prestigious universities such as Columbia University and NYU.

About the reviewer

Xun (Brian) Wu is the Founder and CEO of smartchart.tech. He has over 16 years of extensive hands-on experience in design and development with Blockchain, big data, Cloud, UI, and system infrastructure. He is the coauthor of *Blockchain By Example*, *Hyperledger cookbook*, *Blockchain Quick Start Guide*, and *Seven NoSQL Databases in a Week*. He has also been a technical reviewer for over 40 books for Packt. He served as a board advisor for several blockchain startups and owned several patents on blockchain. He holds a Master's in computer science from NJIT and lives in New Jersey with his two beautiful daughters, Bridget and Charlotte.

> *I would like to thank my parents, wife, and kids for their patience and support throughout this endeavor.*

Nikita Rokotyan is a data visualization engineer with a background in physics and creative technologies. He specializes in creating enriched, data-driven experiences with strong dynamic and interactive components.

Focusing on aesthetics and information content, Nikita has worked on a number of applied and artistic data visualizations for various startups as well as large organizations such as University of Tokyo, Proctor & Gamble, and the Paul Mellon Centre for Studies in British Art.

Currently he's running a data visualization studio Interacta and co-running a company in NYC—CultivateMe—that explores how data visualization can help with a better understanding and cultivating human talent

Packt is searching for authors like you

If you're interested in becoming an author for Packt, please visit `authors.packtpub.com` and apply today. We have worked with thousands of developers and tech professionals, just like you, to help them share their insight with the global tech community. You can make a general application, apply for a specific hot topic that we are recruiting an author for, or submit your own idea.

Table of Contents

Preface

Welcome to *D3.js Quick Start Guide*. In it, we'll be covering the basics of D3 through a series of large builds. By the end, you should have a strong enough grasp of the library to go out and build your own interactive data visualizations.

Who this book is for

This book is for junior-to senior-level frontend and full-stack web developers who are interested in getting to data visualization. The reader needs to have a basic understanding of HTML, CSS, JavaScript, AJAX, and what a server is, in order to be able to work with the code and concepts given in this book.

What this book covers

Chapter 1, *Getting Started with D3.js*, provides a high-level overview of what makes D3 so interesting. We examine what an SVG element is and set up our machine so that it is ready to create D3 code. We also take a look at this book's approach to learning and how it applies to the applications that we'll build.

Chapter 2, *Using SVG to Create Images Using Code*, covers the basics of SVG (base tags, basic elements, positioning, and styling). We also look at Bezier curves and how to draw organic shapes with them. We're now ready to learn how D3 can be used to modify these elements.

Chapter 3, *Building an Interactive Scatter Plot*, explains static scatter plots and a shows how to build a table that displays its data.

Chapter 4, *Making a Basic Scatter Plot Interactive*, shows you as many useful modules as possible, with examples of daily activities that can be carried out and personal comments based on our experience of using them.

Chapter 5, *Create a Bar Graph Using a Data File*, covers many interesting use cases that any system administrator will need to run daily. Many other tasks can be performed as we show with customized playbooks. But not every script is considered as good automation. What matters is that the right nodes go from state A to state B with no errors and in a short time.

Chapter 6, *Animating SVG Elements to Create an Interactive Pie Chart*, shows how a pie chart animates when you remove sections from it.

Chapter 7, *Use Physics to Create a Force Directed Graph*, shows how to use D3 to create a graph that visualizes relationships between various nodes of data. This can be very useful in scenarios such as graphing a friend network, showing parent/child company relationships, or displaying a company's staff hierarchy.

Chapter 8, *Mapping*, discusses GeoJSON, what it's used for, and why it differs from more general JSON data. We also cover how to use D3 to create a projection and render GeoJSON data as a map.

To get the most out of this book

This book assumes a basic understanding of HTML, CSS, JavaScript, AJAX, and what a server is, in order to be able to work with the code and concepts given in this book.

For this book you really only need to download and install the following:

- Chrome, available at https://www.google.com/chrome/: a web browser so that we can view our visualizations.
- Node: https://nodejs.org/en/: This allows us to run JavaScript from the terminal. In Chapter 4, *Making a Basic Scatter Plot Interactive*, we will use it so that we can make AJAX calls.
- A code editor. I'd suggest Atom if you're new to coding: https://atom.io/.

Download the example code files

You can download the example code files for this book from your account at www.packt.com. If you purchased this book elsewhere, you can visit www.packt.com/support and register to have the files emailed directly to you.

You can download the code files by following these steps:

1. Log in or register at www.packt.com.
2. Select the **SUPPORT** tab.
3. Click on **Code Downloads & Errata**.
4. Enter the name of the book in the **Search** box and follow the onscreen instructions.

Once the file is downloaded, please make sure that you unzip or extract the folder using the latest version of:

- WinRAR/7-Zip for Windows
- Zipeg/iZip/UnRarX for Mac
- 7-Zip/PeaZip for Linux

The code bundle for the book is also hosted on GitHub at https://github.com/PacktPublishing/D3.js-Quick-Start-Guide. In case there's an update to the code, it will be updated on the existing GitHub repository.

We also have other code bundles from our rich catalog of books and videos available at https://github.com/PacktPublishing/. Check them out!

Download the color images

We also provide a PDF file that has color images of the screenshots/diagrams used in this book. You can download it here: https://www.packtpub.com/sites/default/files/downloads/9781789342383_ColorImages.pdf.

Conventions used

There are a number of text conventions used throughout this book.

CodeInText: Indicates code words in text, database table names, folder names, filenames, file extensions, pathnames, dummy URLs, user input, and Twitter handles. Here is an example: "Mount the downloaded WebStorm-10*.dmg disk image file as another disk in your system."

A block of code is set as follows:

```
<circle r=50 cx=50 cy=50 fill=red stroke=blue stroke-width=5></circle>
```

When we wish to draw your attention to a particular part of a code block, the relevant lines or items are set in bold:

```
<head>
        <link rel="stylesheet" href="app.css">
</head>
```

Bold: Indicates a new term, an important word, or words that you see onscreen. For example, words in menus or dialog boxes appear in the text like this. Here is an example: "Select **System info** from the **Administration** panel."

Warnings or important notes appear like this.

Tips and tricks appear like this.

Get in touch

Feedback from our readers is always welcome.

General feedback: If you have questions about any aspect of this book, mention the book title in the subject of your message and email us at customercare@packtpub.com.

Errata: Although we have taken every care to ensure the accuracy of our content, mistakes do happen. If you have found a mistake in this book, we would be grateful if you would report this to us. Please visit www.packt.com/submit-errata, selecting your book, clicking on the Errata Submission Form link, and entering the details.

Piracy: If you come across any illegal copies of our works in any form on the Internet, we would be grateful if you would provide us with the location address or website name. Please contact us at copyright@packt.com with a link to the material.

If you are interested in becoming an author: If there is a topic that you have expertise in and you are interested in either writing or contributing to a book, please visit authors.packtpub.com.

Reviews

Please leave a review. Once you have read and used this book, why not leave a review on the site that you purchased it from? Potential readers can then see and use your unbiased opinion to make purchase decisions, we at Packt can understand what you think about our products, and our authors can see your feedback on their book. Thank you!

For more information about Packt, please visit packtpub.com.

Getting Started with D3.js 1

The era of big data is upon us! Advances in hardware have made it possible for computers to store, analyze, and transmit massive amounts of information in a way that was previously impossible. Data science has become one of the most in-demand fields in the United States, and companies are constantly coming up with new techniques to analyze customer information; it seems as if every day there are new ways to visualize all this data. **D3** has become the most popular library used to create dynamic, interactive, data-driven visualizations on the web. Unlike many technologies previously used in data vizualization , D3 leverages the power of combining SVG images with web browsers and JavaScript. In this chapter, we'll discuss the following topics:

- What is SVG?
- What makes D3 so special?
- This book's approach to learning

What is SVG?

One of the best ways to present your data is via an interactive graphic on the web. The advantage of this approach is that its interactivity allows creators to pack more information into a single visualization, while the ubiquity of the web allows anyone to instantly access it. Gone are the days of PowerPoint presentations, or, worse still, printing static images on to paper as handouts. There are many ways to create a web-based interactive data visualization, but none of them is more popular than the JavaScript library called **D3.js**.

To understand why `D3.js` works so well, it's important to understand what SVG is and how it relates to D3. **SVG** stands for **Scalable Vector Graphics**, and it's a way to display shapes using mathematical directions/commands. Traditionally, the information for an image is stored in a grid, also called a raster. Each square (called a pixel) of the image has a specific color:

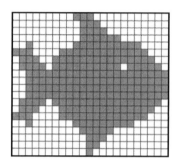

But with SVG, a set of succinct drawing directions is stored. For example, the drawing command for a circle is as follows:

```
<circle r=50><circle>
```

This code produces a much smaller file size, and because it's a set of drawing directions, the image can be enlarged without any pixelation. A raster image becomes blurry and pixelated as it's enlarged. The advantage of raster graphics over vector graphics is that they're great for storing complex images such as photographs. With a photograph, where each pixel probably has a different color, it's better to use a raster image. Imagine writing SVG drawing commands for a photograph: you would end up creating a new element for each pixel, and the file size would be too large.

Once an SVG drawing command is written, a program needs to interpret the command and display the image. Up until recently, only designated drawing applications such as Adobe Illustrator could view and manipulate these images. But by 2011 all major modern browsers supported SVG tags, allowing for developers to embed SVG directly on a web page. Since the SVG image was directly embedded in the code of a web page, JavaScript, which normally is used for manipulating HTML, could be used to manipulate the shape, size, and colors of the image in response to user events. To make the circle in the SVG example you have just seen grow to twice its original size, all that JavaScript had to do was change the rattribute:

```
<circle r=100><circle>
```

This was the massive breakthrough that allowed complex interactive data visualizations to be hosted on the web.

What makes D3 so special?

D3.js came in at this point because writing the code to make complex data-driven documents (how D3 got its name) that linked SVG images with the big data that had become available on the internet was a difficult task. It rose to prominence during the Obama/Romney presidential debates as the New York times published a series of amazing visualizations. Check out some examples here:

- https://archive.nytimes.com/www.nytimes.com/interactive/2012/11/07/us/politics/obamas-diverse-base-of-support.html
- http://archive.nytimes.com/www.nytimes.com/interactive/2012/11/02/us/politics/paths-to-the-white-house.html
- https://archive.nytimes.com/www.nytimes.com/interactive/2012/10/15/us/politics/swing-history.html
- https://www.nytimes.com/elections/2012/electoral-map.html
- https://archive.nytimes.com/www.nytimes.com/interactive/2012/09/06/us/politics/convention-word-counts.html
- https://archive.nytimes.com/www.nytimes.com/interactive/2012/03/07/us/politics/how-candidates-fared-with-different-demographic-groups.html

D3 simplifies some of the most common, as well as some of the most, complex tasks that a developer can run into when creating browser-based visualizations. At its core, D3 easily maps SVG image properties to data values. As the data values change, due to user interactions, so do the images.

This book's approach to learning

D3 is a massive library, full of millions of options, but its core concepts are easy to learn. You do not need to know every detail of the library to become a functional D3 developer. Instead, this book attempts to teach the most fundamental aspects of D3 so that the reader can get job-ready quickly. It does so by stepping the user through a series of the most common graphs that a developer will be asked to make: a scatter plot, a bar graph, a pie chart, a force-directed graph, and a map. The goal is not only to teach the basics but also to give the reader a final set of builds that are fun to work, toward as well as useful to draw from as their career continues.

Please note, the code demonstrated here was created to be easy to understand from an educational standpoint. It is not meant to be code that is ready for production. Nor does it employ ES6 or ES7 syntax. Often, demonstrating a concept in code that is production-ready or written in ES6/ES7 can hinder the educational experience. It is assumed that the reader is comfortable enough with the core concepts of programming that they can refine the code on their own, once they are comfortable with the fundamentals of D3.

A preview of each build

Each chapter focuses on a specific build. The completed build code for each chapter can be found at: https://github.com/PacktPublishing/D3.js-Quick-Start-Guide.

Using SVG to create images using code

In this chapter, we learn how to render shapes in the browser, using SVG. We'll cover shapes such as these:

- Circles:

- Lines:

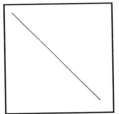

- Rectangles:

- Ellipses:

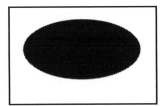

- Polygons:

- Polylines:

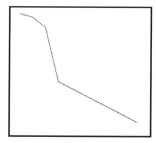

- Cubic Bezier Curves:

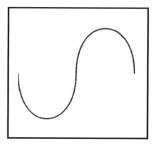

The completed code for this section can be found here: `https://github.com/PacktPublishing/D3.js-Quick-Start-Guide/tree/master/Chapter02`.

Building an interactive scatter plot

In this chapter, you'll learn how to plot points on a graph to create a scatter plot. It will look a bit like this:

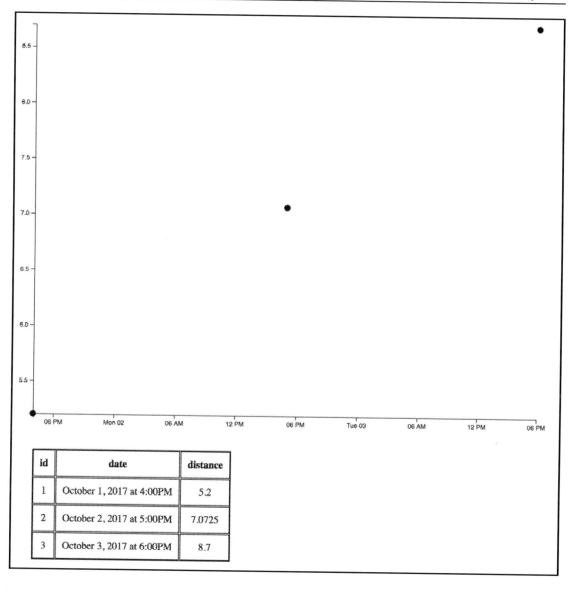

id	date	distance
1	October 1, 2017 at 4:00PM	5.2
2	October 2, 2017 at 5:00PM	7.0725
3	October 3, 2017 at 6:00PM	8.7

The completed code for this section can be found here: `https://github.com/PacktPublishing/D3.js-Quick-Start-Guide/tree/master/Chapter03`.

Making a basic scatter plot interactive

This chapter builds on the previous one, adding interactive functionality that allows you to do the following:

- Create new points:

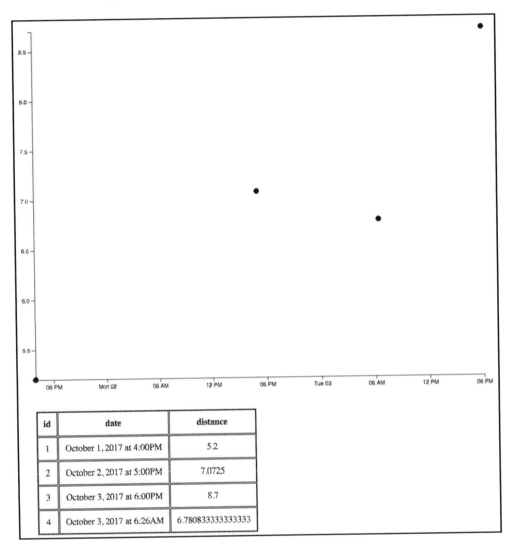

- Remove points:

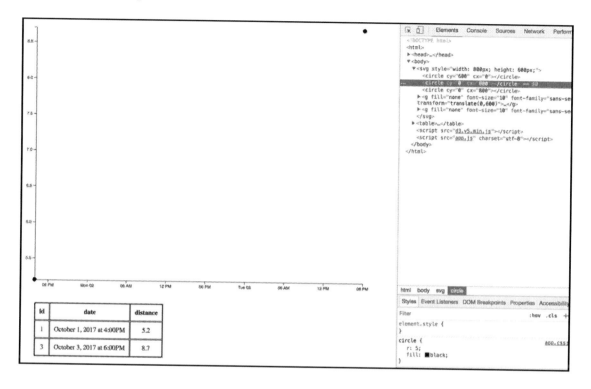

id	date	distance
1	October 1, 2017 at 4:00PM	5.2
3	October 3, 2017 at 6:00PM	8.7

- Update points:

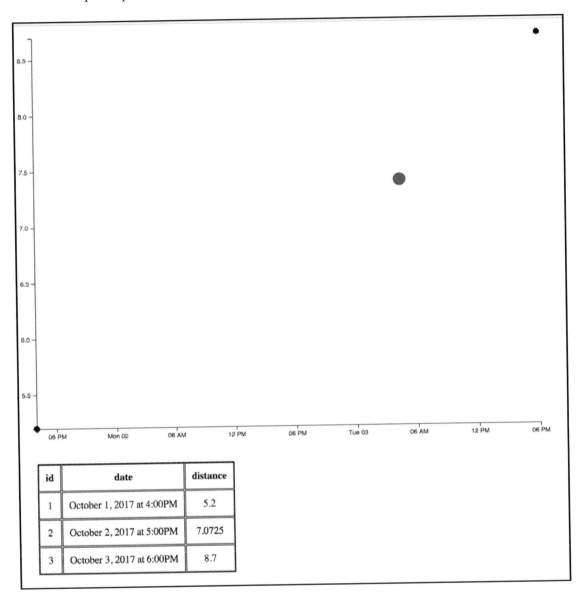

id	date	distance
1	October 1, 2017 at 4:00PM	5.2
2	October 2, 2017 at 5:00PM	7.0725
3	October 3, 2017 at 6:00PM	8.7

- Zoom and pan:

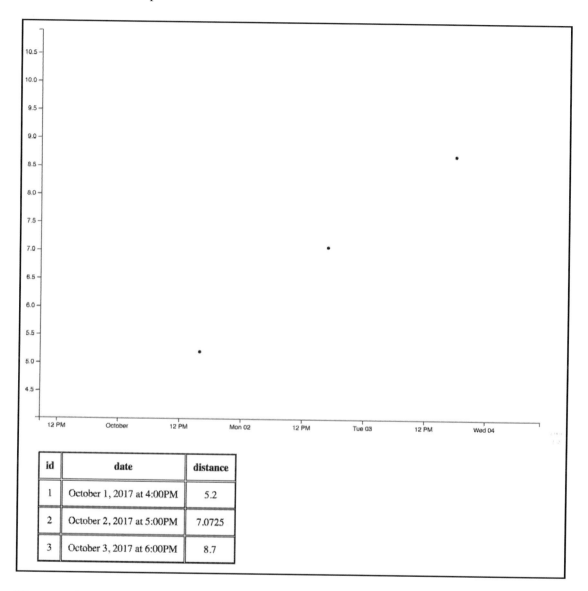

id	date	distance
1	October 1, 2017 at 4:00PM	5.2
2	October 2, 2017 at 5:00PM	7.0725
3	October 3, 2017 at 6:00PM	8.7

The completed code for this section can be found here: `https://github.com/PacktPublishing/D3.js-Quick-Start-Guide/tree/master/Chapter04`.

Creating a bar graph using a data file

In this chapter, we'll learn how to use AJAX to make an asynchronous call, after the page has loaded, to retrieve some JSON data and render it as a bar graph. It should look as follows:

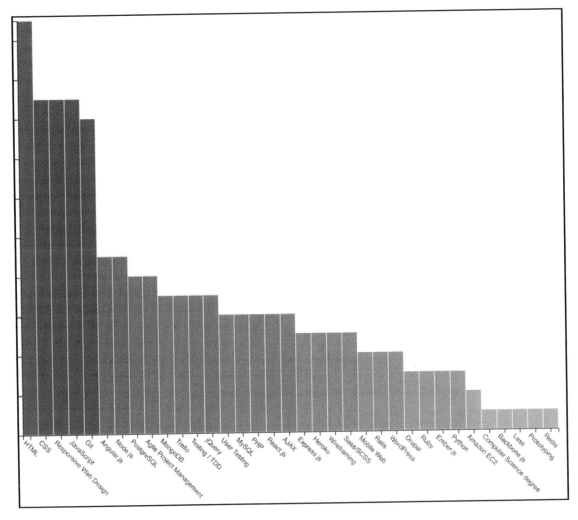

The completed code for this section can be found here: https://github.com/ PacktPublishing/D3.js-Quick-Start-Guide/tree/master/Chapter05.

Animating SVG elements to create an interactive pie chart

In this chapter, we'll learn how to make a pie chart:

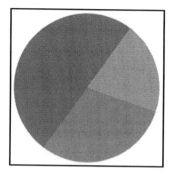

Then we'll turn it into a donut chart:

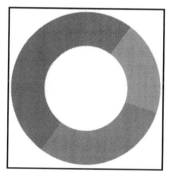

And then we'll create functionality so that the user can remove a section of the chart and it will close the gap with a smooth transition:

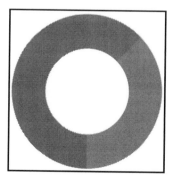

The completed code for this section can be found here: `https://github.com/PacktPublishing/D3.js-Quick-Start-Guide/tree/master/Chapter06`.

Using physics to create a force-directed graph

In this chapter, we'll graph relationships between people with a force-directed graph. It will look as follows:

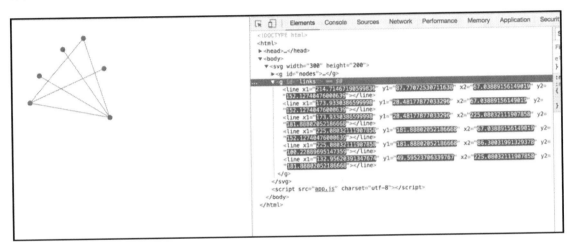

The completed code for this section can be found here: `https://github.com/PacktPublishing/D3.js-Quick-Start-Guide/tree/master/Chapter07`.

Mapping

In `Chapter 8`, *Mapping*, we'll learn how to use GeoJSON data to create a map of the world. It will look as follows:

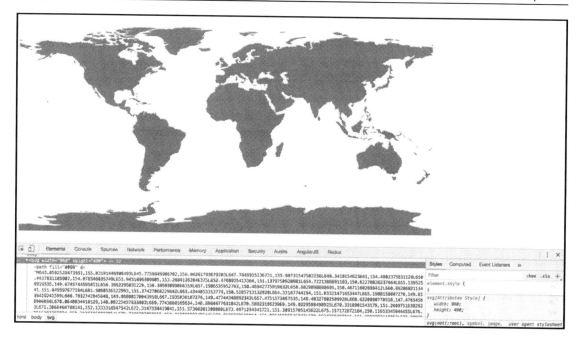

The completed code for this section can be found here: `https://github.com/PacktPublishing/D3.js-Quick-Start-Guide/tree/master/Chapter08`.

Setting up

For this book, you really only need to download and install the following:

- Chrome: `https://www.google.com/chrome/`.
    - A web browser so that we can view our visualizations.
- Node: `https://nodejs.org/en/`.
    - This allows us to run javascript from the terminal. In `Chapter 4`, *Making a Basic Scatter Plot Interactive*, we will use it so that we can make AJAX calls.
- A code editor. I'd suggest Atom if you're new to coding: `https://atom.io/`.

Summary

In this chapter, you've received a high-level overview of what makes D3 so interesting. We examined what an SVG element is and set up our machine so that it is ready to create D3 code. We also took a look at this book's approach to learning and how it applies to the applications that we'll build. In Chapter 2, *Using SVG to Create Images Using Code*, we'll dive into creating SVG elements.

2
Using SVG to Create Images Using Code

SVG elements are a way to create images within a web page and are the foundation of D3 and how it works. They use code to create shapes, rather than defining each pixel of an image. This chapter covers how to create various SVG elements within a web page. In it, we will cover the following topics:

- Base tags
- Basic elements
- Positioning
- Styling
- Important SVG elements

The complete code for this section can be found here: `https://github.com/PacktPublishing/D3.js-Quick-Start-Guide/tree/master/Chapter02`.

Base tag

When viewing SVG graphics in a browser, it's important to embed an `<svg>` tag inside an HTML page. Let's create an `index.html` file and add the following to it:

```
<!DOCTYPE html>
<html lang="en" dir="ltr">
    <head>
    </head>
    <body>
        <svg></svg>
    </body>
</html>
```

Now start a web browser and open that file (usually, **File** | **Open File**). For this book, it is recommended that the reader use Google Chrome, but in development and production, any browser will do. If we inspect our HTML in the **Elements** tab of Chrome's Dev Tools (**View** | **Developer** | **Developer Tools**), we'll see the following:

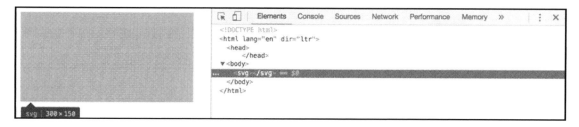

Basic elements

We can draw elements in our \<svg\> element by adding a variety of predefined tags as child elements of the \<svg\>. This is just as we did in HTML, where we add \<div\>, \<a\>, and \<img\> tags inside the \<body\> tag. There are many tags, such as \<circle\>, \<rect\>, and \<line\>, that we'll explore in a bit. Here's just one example:

```
<!DOCTYPE html>
<html lang="en" dir="ltr">
    <head>
    </head>
    <body>
        <svg>
            <circle></circle>
        </svg>
    </body>
</html>
```

Note that we can't see the circle because it doesn't have a radius, as shown in this screenshot:

We'll talk more about this later, but, for now, if we want to see the circle, we can add a special attribute that all `<circle>` elements take:

```
<circle r=50></circle>
```

This tells the browser to give the circle a radius of 50 px, which is shown in the following screenshot:

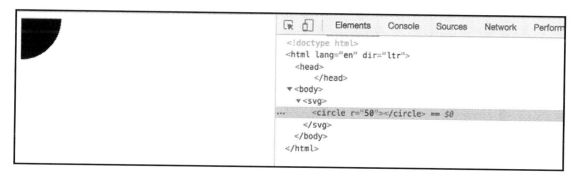

At the moment, though, we only see the lower–right quarter of the circle. This is because the center of the circle is being drawn at the very upper–left corner of the `<svg>`, and the rest of it is being clipped outside the `<svg>`. We can change this by changing the position of the circle, which we'll do next.

Positioning an element

The `<svg>` tag is an inline element, such as an image (as opposed to a block element such as a `<div>`). Elements within the `<svg>` are positioned similar to Photoshop, with a set of coordinates that follow the form `(x,y)`. An example of this could be `(10,15)`, which translates to x=10 and y=15. This is different than HTML, where elements are laid out relative to one another. Here are some important things to keep in mind:

- The point `(0,0)` is the upper–left corner of the `<svg>` element.
- As *y* values increase, the point moves vertically down the `<svg>` element.
- Don't confuse this with a typical coordinate system that has `(0,0)` at the lower–left corner with a point moving up, as *y* increases in value. This diagram shows the difference between a traditional coordinate system and an SVG coordinate system:

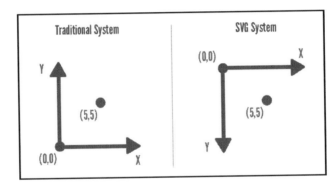

We can use negative *x/y* values:

- -*x*: moves left
- -*y* :moves up

Let's adjust the position of our circle in our previous section by adjusting `cx` and `cy` values (the *x* and *y* values for the center of the element):

```
<!DOCTYPE html>
<html lang="en" dir="ltr">
    <head>
    </head>
    <body>
        <svg>
            <circle r=50 cx=50 cy=50></circle>
        </svg>
```

```
    </body>
</html>
```

Now we see the full circle:

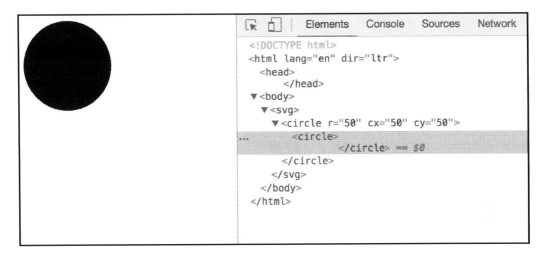

Styling an element

The appearance of any tag inside an `<svg>` can be styled with the following attributes (the following are the attributes with example values):

- `fill=red` or `fill=#ff0000` will alter the color of the shape.
- `stroke=red` or `stroke=#ff0000` will alter stroke color. Stroke is a line that surrounds each element.
- `stroke-width=4` will adjust the width of the stroke.
- `fill-opacity=0.5` will adjust the transparency of the fill color.
- `stroke-opacity=0.5` will adjust the transparency of the stroke color.
- `transform = "translate(2,3)"` will translate the element by the given x, y values.
- `transform = "scale(2.1)"` will scale the size of the element by the given proportion (for example, `2.1` times as big).
- `transform = "rotate(45)"` will rotate the element by the given number of degrees.

Let's style the circle we positioned previously:

```
<circle r=50 cx=50 cy=50 fill=red stroke=blue stroke-width=5></circle>
```

Now we get this:

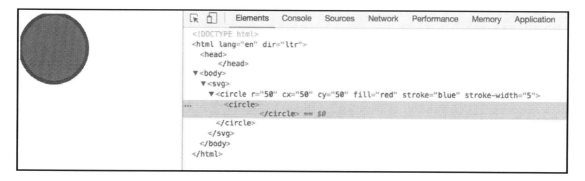

Note that the stroke in the preceding screenshot is getting clipped. That's because the stroke is created outside the element. If we want to see the full stroke, we can resize the circle:

```
<circle r=45 cx=50 cy=50 fill=red stroke=blue stroke-width=5></circle>
```

Now we get the following output:

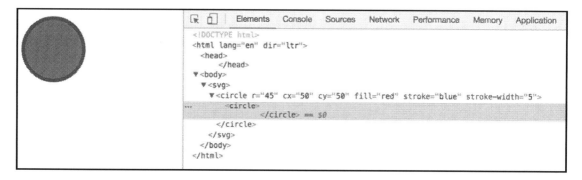

Styling can also be done with CSS. The following steps will tell you how to style your `<svg>` element with CSS:

1. Create an external `app.css` file in the same folder as your `index.html` file with the following contents:

```
circle {
    fill:red;
    stroke:blue;
```

```
    stroke-width:3;
    fill-opacity:0.5;
    stroke-opacity:0.1;
    transform:rotate(45deg) scale(0.4) translate(155px,
    1px);
    r:50px;
}
```

2. Link the file in the `<head>` tag of `index.html`:

```
<head> <link rel="stylesheet" href="app.css"> </head>
```

3. Lastly, remove our previous inline styling that we had on our `<circle>` tag:

```
<circle></circle>
```

Now we get this result:

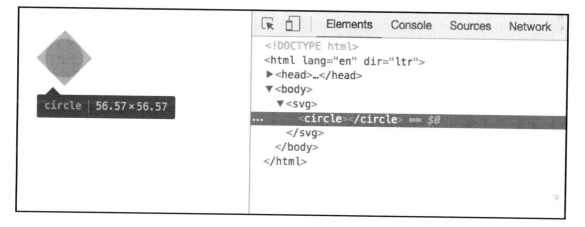

Note that I've hovered over the element in the dev tools to show that the element has been rotated 45 degrees. That's what the blue box is.

Important SVG elements

To demonstrate each element, we'll use the following code as a starting point and then add each element inside the `<svg>` tag:

```
<!DOCTYPE html>
<html lang="en" dir="ltr">
    <head>
    </head>
    <body>
        <svg width=800 height=600>
        </svg>
    </body>
</html>
```

Let's now move on to each element. Note that you can write each tag in the form `<element></element>`, as we did with `<circle></circle>` previously, or the self-closing form, `<element/>`, which you will see next with `<circle/>`.

Circle

Circles have the following attributes:

- r: radius
- cx: *x* position
- cy: *y* position

```
<circle r="50" cx="200" cy="300"/>
```

The output for the previous code will be as follows:

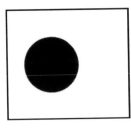

Line

Lines have the following attributes:

- x1: starting x position
- y1: starting y position
- x2: ending x position
- y2: ending y position

Here are two examples:

```
<!--
the first element won't be visible because it doesn't have a stroke
the second will be visible because it does have a stroke
-->
<line x1="0" y1="0" x2="100" y2="100"/>
<line x1="0" y1="0" x2="100" y2="100" stroke="purple"/>
```

The following output will be displayed:

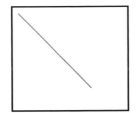

Rectangle

Rectangles have the following attributes:

- x: x position of upper–left
- y: y position of top left
- width: width
- height: height

Here's an example:

```
<rect x="50" y="20" width="150" height="150"/>
```

Here's what this code produces:

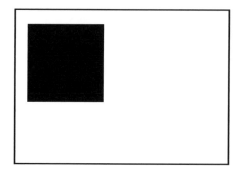

Ellipse

An ellipse has the following attributes:

- cx: *x* position
- cy: *y* position
- rx: *x* radius
- ry: *y* radius

The attributes will be as follows:

```
<ellipse cx="200" cy="80" rx="100" ry="50"/>
```

The output can be seen as follows:

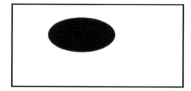

Polygon

Polygons have the following attributes:

- points, which is a set of coordinate pairs
- Each pair is of the form x, y

The attributes will be as follows:

```
<polygon points="200,10 250,190 160,210" />
```

The output can be seen as follows:

Polyline

Polyline is a series of connected lines. It can have a fill, as a polygon does, but it won't automatically rejoin itself:

```
<polyline points="20,20 40,25 60,40 80,120 120,140 200,180" stroke="blue"
fill="none"/>
```

The output will be as follows:

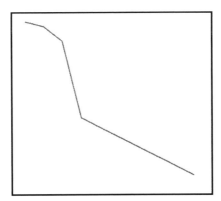

Text

The content of the tag is the text to be displayed. It has the following attributes:

- x, the *x* position of upper–left corner of the element
- y, the *y* position of upper-left corner of the element

The attributes can be used as follows:

```
<text x="0" y="15">I love SVG!</text>
```

You can use `font-family` and `font-size` CSS styling on this element.

Group

This element has no special attributes, so we'll use transform to position it. You can put multiple elements inside it and all of its positioning will apply to its children. It's good for moving many elements together as one:

```
<g transform = "translate(20,30) rotate(45) scale(0.5)"></g>
```

Bezier curves

What if we want to draw complex organic shapes? To do this, we'll need to use paths. First, though, to understand paths, you have to understand **Bezier curves**.

Cubic Bezier curves

There are two types of Bezier curves:

- Bezier curves (`http://blogs.sitepointstatic.com/examples/tech/svg-curves/cubic-curve.html`)
- Quadratic Bezier curves (`http://math.hws.edu/eck/cs424/notes2013/canvas/bezier.html`)

Each curve is made up of four points:

- Start point
- End point
- Starting control point
- Ending control point

The start/end points are where the curve starts and ends. The control points define the shape of the curve. It's easiest to conceptualize it with the following diagram:

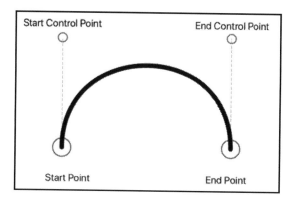

As we manipulate the control points, we can see how the shape of the curve is affected:

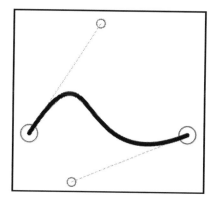

You can even join multiple Bezier curves together, as shown in this diagram:

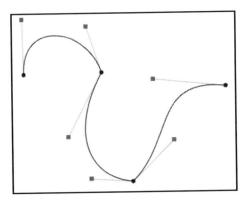

Smooth cubic Bezier curves

Smooth cubic Bezier curves are just a way to simplify some cubic Bezier curves when they're joined together. Take a look at the two control points in the red square shown in this diagram:

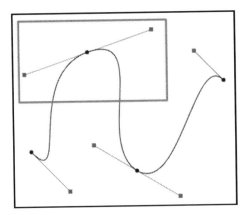

The point in the lower–left corner of the square is the end control point of the first curve. The point in the upper-right corner of the square is start control point of the second curve.

Note that the two points are reflections of each other around the central black dot, which is the end point of the first curve and the start point of the second curve. The two points are exactly 180 degrees from each other, and they have the same distance from that central point.

In scenarios such as this, where the start control point of one curve is a reflection of the end control point of the previous curve, we can skip stating the start control point of the second curve. Instead, we let the browser calculate it, based on the end control point of the first curve:

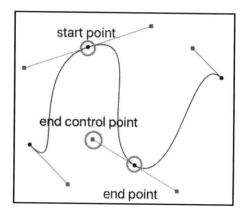

We can also omit the start point, since the browser knows it will be the same as the end point of the previous curve. In summary, to define that second curve, we only need two points:

- The end point
- The end control point

Quadratic Bezier curve

Another situation where we can simplify defining a Bezier curve is where the start control point and end control point are the same:

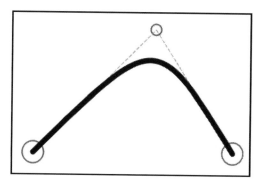

Here, we can define the curve with just three points:

- The start point
- The end point
- One single control point that acts as both a start control point and an end control point

Smooth quadratic Bezier curve

The final situation where we can simplify defining a Bezier curve is where we have a quadratic Bezier curve (one single control point) that is a reflection of the end control point of a previous curve:

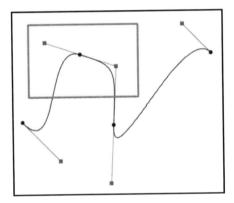

In this situation, the browser knows the start point of the curve (the end point of the previous curve), and it can calculate the single control point needed (since it is a quadratic Bezier curve) based on the end control point of the previous curve. This is a smooth quadratic Bezier curve, and you only need one point to define it:

- The end point

Drawing a path

Now that we understand Bezier curves, we can use them in our SVGs with <path> elements.

Documentation can be found here: `https://developer.mozilla.org/en-US/docs/Web/SVG/Tutorial/Paths`.

These tags take a d attribute, which stands for a set of drawing commands. The value of this attribute is any combination of the following:

- M = moveto: move the drawing point to the given coordinates
    - M *x y*
- L = lineto: draw a line from the previous point in the d command to the point given
    - L *x y*
- C = curveto: draw a curve from the previous point in the d command to the point given with the given control points
    - C *x1 y1, x2 y2, x y*
    - The first pair is first control point
    - The second pair is second control point
    - The last pair is final ending point of curve
- S = smooth curveto:
    - S *x2 y2, x y*
    - Follows another curve
    - Uses a reflection of *x2 y2* of the previous S or C command for *x1 y1*
- Q = quadratic Bezier curve:
    - Q *x1 y1, x y*
    - Uses one control point for start and end controls (*x1, y1*)
- T = smooth quadratic Bezier curveto:
    - T *x y*
    - Follows another curve
    - Uses a reflection of the previous quadratic curve's control point as its control point
- Z = closepath: draws a line from the previous point in the d command to the first point in the d command

Note that all of these commands can also be expressed with lowercase letters. If capital letters are used, this means absolutely positioned (relative to the upper-left corner of the SVG element); lowercase letters mean that all the points are expressed relative to the previous point in the d command.

Let's use lines to draw a triangle:

```
<path d="M150 0 L75 200 L225 200 Z" stroke="black" fill="transparent"/>
```

The following output will be displayed:

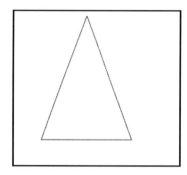

Next, we'll draw a Bezier curve:

```
<path d="M0 70 C 0 120, 50 120, 50 70 S 100 20, 100 70" stroke="black"
fill="transparent"/>
```

The following output will be displayed:

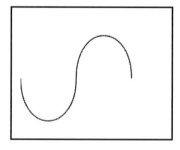

Here's a quadratic Bezier curve:

```
<path d="M0 100 Q 50 50, 100 100 T 200 100 Z" stroke="black"
fill="transparent"/>
```

The following output will be displayed:

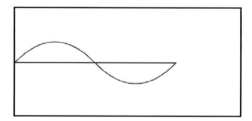

Arcs

An **arc** is a command that you can add to a path that will draw part of an ellipse. To do this, we begin with only two points:

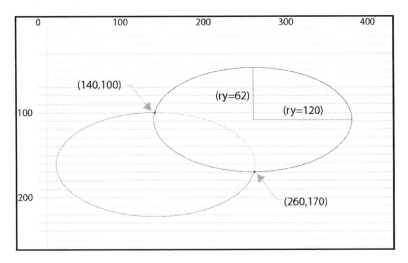

For any two points, there are only two ellipses with the same width/height and rotation that contain both points. In the previous diagram, try to imagine moving the ellipses around without rotating or scaling them. As soon as you do, they lose contact with at least one of the two given points. One point might be on the ellipse, but the other won't be.

We can use this information to draw any of the four colored arcs shown in the previous diagram.

Make the following code part of the d attribute's value on a <path> element:

```
A rx ry x-axis-rotation large-arc-flag sweep-flag x y
```

Let's look at the various properties of an arc:

- A: creates an arc draw command
- rx: the *x* radius of both ellipses (in px)
- ry: the *y* radius of both ellipses (in px)
- x-axis-rotation: rotates both ellipses a certain number of degrees
- large-arc-flag: indicates whether to travel along the arc that contains more than 180 degrees (1 to do so, 0 to not do so)

- `sweep-flag`: indicates whether to move along the arc that goes clockwise (1 to do so, 0 to not do so)
- `x`: destination *x* value (in px)
- `y`: destination *y* value (in px)

`large-arc-flag` determines whether to make an arc that is greater than 180 degrees. Here's an example without it (note, the red shows the arc drawn, while the green arcs are other possible arcs that could be drawn using a combination of `large-arc-flag` and `sweep-flag`):

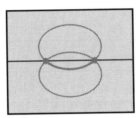

Note, it chooses one of the two smaller arcs. Here's an example with the `large-arc-flag` set:

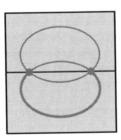

Note, it chooses one of the two larger arcs.

In the previous example, for both situations where the `large-arc-flag` was set or not set, there was one other arc that could have been taken. To determine which of those two arcs to take, we use the `sweep-flag`, which determines whether to travel clockwise from the start point to the end point. Here's an example with the `large-arc-flag` set, but without the `sweep-flag` set:

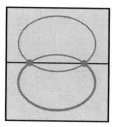

Note that we move in a counterclockwise motion from start to end (left to right). If we set the `sweep-flag`, we travel in a clockwise motion:

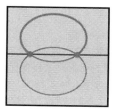

Here are all the possible combinations for `sweep-flag` and `large-arc-flag`:

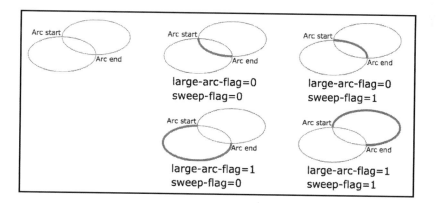

Here's an example code for a `path` that uses an arc in its `d` attribute:

```
<path d="M10 10 A 50 50 0 0 0 50 10" stroke="black" fill="transparent"/>
```

Here's what it looks like:

Play with the different kinds of arc values here: `http://codepen.io/lingtalfi/pen/yaLWJG`.

Documentation

If needed, you can find all the documentation for SVG elements here: `https://developer.mozilla.org/en-US/docs/Web/SVG/Element`.

Summary

In this chapter, we covered the basics of SVG (base tags, basic elements, positioning, and styling). We also looked at Bezier curves and how to draw organic shapes with them. We're now ready to learn how D3 can be used to modify these elements. In `Chapter 3`, *Building an Interactive Scatter Plot*, we will dive into the basics of `D3.js` and create an interactive scatter plot.

Building an Interactive Scatter Plot

3

Let's pretend we've started jogging and we want to visualize the data regarding our progress as a runner, with a scatter plot. We're going to have an array of objects, each with a date and distance properties. For each object in the array, we're going to create a circle in our SVG. If the `distance` property of an object is relatively high, its associated circle will be higher up on the graph. If the `date` property of an object is relatively high (a later date), its associated circle will be farther right.

By the end of this lesson, you should be able to do the following:

- Add a link to the D3 library
- Add an`<svg>`tag and size it with D3
- Create some fake data for our app
- Add SVG circles and style them
- Create a linear scale
- Attach data to visual elements
- Use data attached to a visual element to affect its appearance
- Create a time scale
- Parse and format times
- Set dynamic domains
- Dynamically generate SVG elements
- Create axes
- Display data in a table

The complete code for this section can be found here: `https://github.com/PacktPublishing/D3.js-Quick-Start-Guide/tree/master/Chapter03`.

Adding a link to the D3 library

The first thing we want to do is create a basic `index.html` file:

```
<!DOCTYPE html>
<html>
    <head>
        <meta charset="utf-8">
        <title></title>
    </head>
    <body>
    </body>
</html>
```

Now add a link to D3 at the bottom of your `<body>` tag in `index.html`. We'll put it at the bottom so that the script loads after all your other HTML elements have loaded into the browser:

```
<body>
    <script src="https://d3js.org/d3.v5.min.js"></script>
</body>
```

Now create `app.js` in the same folder as your `index.html`. In it, we will store all of our JS code. For now, just put this code in it to see whether it works:

```
console.log('this works');
console.log(d3);
```

Link to it in `index.html` at the bottom of the `<body>` tag. Make sure it comes after the D3 script tag so that D3 loads before your `app.js` script:

```
<body>
    <script src="https://d3js.org/d3.v5.min.js"></script>
    <script src="app.js" charset="utf-8"></script>
</body>
```

Open `index.html` in Chrome just as we did in Chapter 2, *Using SVG to Create Images Using Code*, (**File** | **Open File**), and check your Dev Tools (**View** | **Developer** | **Developer tools**) to see whether your JavaScript files are linked correctly:

```
this works                          app.js:1
                                    app.js:2

▼ Object 🔘
  ▶ active: ƒ (t,n)
  ▶ arc: ƒ ()
  ▶ area: ƒ Mf()
  ▶ areaRadial: ƒ Cf()
  ▶ ascending: ƒ n(t,n)
  ▶ axisBottom: ƒ (t)
  ▶ axisLeft: ƒ (t)
  ▶ axisRight: ƒ (t)
  ▶ axisTop: ƒ (t)
  ▶ bisect: ƒ (n,e,r,i)
  ▶ bisectLeft: ƒ (n,e,r,i)
  ▶ bisectRight: ƒ (n,e,r,i)
  ▶ bisector: ƒ e(t)
  ▶ blob: ƒ (t,n)
  ▶ brush: ƒ ()
  ▶ brushSelection: ƒ (t)
  ▶ brushX: ƒ ()
  ▶ brushY: ƒ ()
  ▶ buffer: ƒ (t,n)
  ▶ chord: ƒ ()
  ▶ clientPoint: ƒ dt(t,n)
  ▶ cluster: ƒ ()
  ▶ color: ƒ kt(t)
  ▶ contourDensity: ƒ ()
  ▶ contours: ƒ Me()
  ▶ create: ƒ (t)
  ▶ creator: ƒ C(t)
  ▶ cross: ƒ (t,n,e)
  ▶ csv: ƒ (n,e,r)
  ▶ csvFormat: ƒ (n,e)
  ▶ csvFormatRows: ƒ (t)
  ▶ csvParse: ƒ (t,e)
  ▶ csvParseRows: ƒ n(t,n)
  ▶ cubehelix: ƒ Zt(t,n,e,r)
```

Adding an<svg>tag and sizing it with D3

In <indexentry content=" tag:sizing, with D3"> the index.html, at the top of
<body>, before <indexentry content=" tag:adding"> your script tags, add an <svg>
tag:

```
<body>
    <svg></svg>
    <script src="https://d3js.org/d3.v5.min.js"></script>
    <script src="app.js" charset="utf-8"></script>
</body>
```

If we examine the **Elements** tab of our dev tools, we'll <indexentry content=" tag:adding"> see the svg element has <indexentry content=" tag:sizing, with D3"> been placed. In Chrome, it has a default width/height of 300 px/150 px:

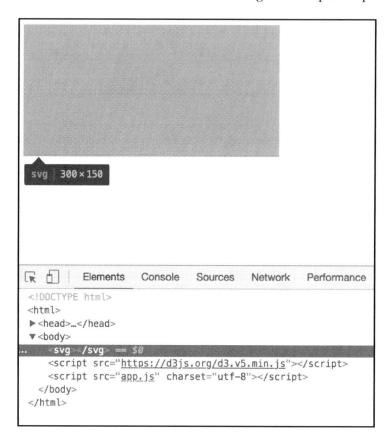

In app.js, remove your previous console.log statements and create variables to hold the width and height of the <svg> tag:

```
var WIDTH = 800;
var HEIGHT = 600;
```

Next, we can use d3.select() to select a single element, in this case the <svg> element:

```
var WIDTH = 800;
var HEIGHT = 600;

d3.select('svg');
```

The return value of d3.select('svg') is a D3 version of the svg element (as in jQuery), so we can chain commands onto this. Let's add some styling to adjust the height/width of the element:

```
d3.select('svg')
    .style('width', WIDTH)
    .style('height', HEIGHT);
```

Now, when we check the dev tools, we'll see the <svg> element has been resized:

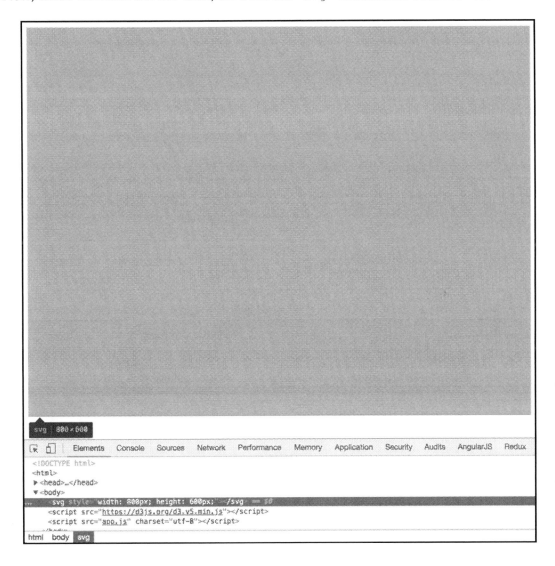

Creating some fake data for our app

In `app.js`, let's create an array of `run` objects, I am storing the date as a string on purpose also, it's important that this is an array of objects, to work with D3). Here's what your `app.js` code should look like so far:

```
var WIDTH = 800;
var HEIGHT = 600;

var runs = [
    {
        id: 1,
        date: 'October 1, 2017 at 4:00PM',
        distance: 5.2
    },
    {
        id: 2,
        date: 'October 2, 2017 at 5:00PM',
        distance: 7.0725
    },
    {
        id: 3,
        date: 'October 3, 2017 at 6:00PM',
        distance: 8.7
    }
];

d3.select('svg')
    .style('width', WIDTH)
    .style('height', HEIGHT);
```

Adding SVG circles and styling them

In `index.html`, add three circles to your `<svg>` element (each one will represent a run):

```
<svg>
    <circle/>
    <circle/>
    <circle/>
</svg>
```

Create `app.css` in the same folder as `index.html`, with some styling for the circles and our `svg` element:

```
circle {
    r:5;
    fill: black;
}
svg {
    border: 1px solid black;
}
```

Link to it in the head of `index.html`:

```
<head>
    <meta charset="utf-8">
    <title></title>
    <link rel="stylesheet" href="app.css">
</head>
```

Our page should now look as follows:

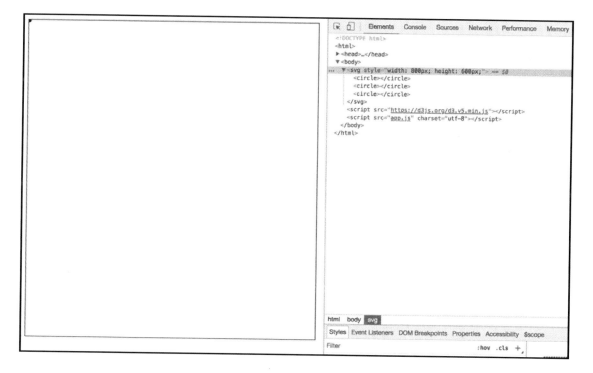

Creating a linear scale

We currently have three circles in our SVG and three objects in our runs array. One of the best things D3 does is provide the ability to link SVG elements with data so that as the data changes so do the SVG elements. In this chapter, we're going to link each circle to an object in the runs array. If the distance property of an object is relatively high, its associated circle will be higher up on the graph. If the date property of an object is relatively high (a later date), its associated circle is farther right.

First, let's position the circles vertically, based on the distance property of the objects in our runs array. One of the most important things that D3 does is provide the ability to convert (or map) data values to visual points and vice versa. It does so using a scale. There are lots of different kinds of scales that handle lots of different data types, but for now we're just going to use a linear scale, which will map numeric data values to numeric visual points, and vice versa.

At the bottom of app.js, add the following:

```
var yScale = d3.scaleLinear(); //create the scale
```

Whenever we create a scale, we need to tell it the minimum and maximum possible values that can exist in our data (this is called the domain). To do so for our yScale, add the following to the bottom of app.js:

```
yScale.domain([0, 10]); //minimum data value is 0, max is 10
```

We also need to tell the scale what visual values correspond to those min/max values in the data (this is called the range). To do so, add the following to the bottom of app.js:

```
//HEIGHT corresponds to min data value
//0 corresponds to max data value
yScale.range([HEIGHT, 0]);
```

Your last three lines of code in app.js should now look as follows:

```
var yScale = d3.scaleLinear(); //create the scale
yScale.domain([0, 10]); //minimum data value is 0, max is 10
//HEIGHT corresponds to min data value
//0 corresponds to max data value
yScale.range([HEIGHT, 0]);
```

In the previous snippet, the first (starting) value for the range is HEIGHT (600) and the second (ending) value is 0. The minimum for the data values is 0 and the max is 10. By doing this, we're saying that a data point (distance run) of 0 should map to a visual height value of HEIGHT (600):

```
var yScale = d3.scaleLinear(); //
yScale.range([HEIGHT, 0]); //set
yScale.domain([0, 10]); //set the
```

This is because the lower the distance run (data value), the more we want to move the visual point down the *y* axis. Remember that the *y* axis starts with 0 at the top and increases in value as we move down vertically on the screen.

We also say that a data point (distance run) of 10 should map to a visual height of 0:

```
var yScale = d3.scaleLinear(); //create the scale
yScale.range([HEIGHT, 0]); //set the visual range (e.g. 600 to 0)
yScale.domain([0, 10]); //set the data domain (e.g. 0 to 10)
```

Again, this is because, as the distance run increases, we want to get back a visual value that is lower and lower so that our circles are closer to the top of the screen.

If you ever need to remind yourself what the domain/range is, you can do so by logging yScale.domain() or yScale.range(). Temporarily add the following at the bottom app.js:

```
//you can get the domain whenever you want like this
console.log(yScale.domain());
//you can get the range whenever you want like this:
console.log(yScale.range());
```

Our Chrome console should look as follows:

```
▶ (2) [0, 10]
▶ (2) [600, 0]
```

When declaring the range/domain of a linear scale, we only need to specify start/end values for each. Values in between the start/end will be calculated by D3. For instance, to find out what visual value corresponds to the distance value of 5, use `yScale()`. Remove the previous two `console.log()` statements and add the following to the bottom of `app.js`:

```
console.log(yScale(5)); //get a visual point from a data value
```

Here's what our dev console should look like in Chrome:

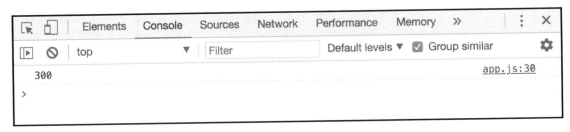

It makes sense that this logs `300` because the data value of `5` is half way between the minimum data value of `0` and the maximum data value of `10`. The range starts at `HEIGHT` (600) and goes to `0`, so halfway between those values is 300.

So, whenever you want to convert a data point to a visual point, call `yScale()`. We can go the other way and convert a visual point to a data value by calling `yScale.invert()`. To find out what data point corresponds to a visual value of 450, remove the previous `console.log()` statement and add the following to the bottom of `app.js`:

```
//get a data values from a visual point
console.log(yScale.invert(450));
```

Here's what Chrome's console looks like:

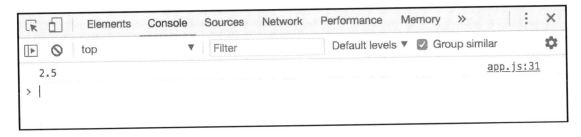

It makes sense that this logs 2.5 because the visual value of 450 is 25% of the way from the starting visual value of 600 (HEIGHT)to the ending visual value of 0. You can now delete that last console.log() line.

Attaching data to visual elements

Now let's attach each of the JavaScript objects in our runs array to a circle in our SVG. Once we do this, each circle can access the data of its associated run object to determine its position. Add the following to the bottom of app.js:

```
yScale.range([HEIGHT, 0]);
yScale.domain([0, 10]);
//selectAll is like select,
//but it selects all elements that match the query string
d3.selectAll('circle').data(runs);
```

If there were more objects in our runs array than there are circles, the extra objects are ignored. If there are more circles than objects, then JavaScript objects are attached to circles in the order in which they appear in the DOM until there are no more objects to attach.

Use data attached to a visual element to affect its appearance

We can change attributes for a selection of DOM elements by passing static values, and all selected elements will have that attribute set to that one specific value. Add the following temporarily to the end of app.js:

```
d3.selectAll('circle').attr('cy', 300);
```

The following should be seen on your screen:

But now that each circle has one of our `runs` JavaScript data objects attached to it, we can set attributes on each circle using that data. We do that by passing the `.attr()` method a callback function instead of a static value for its second parameter. Remove `d3.selectAll('circle').attr('cy', 300);` and adjust the last line of `app.js` from `d3.selectAll('circle').data(runs);` to the following:

```
d3.selectAll('circle').data(runs)
    .attr('cy', function(datum, index){
        return yScale(datum.distance);
    });
```

If we refresh the browser, this is what we should see:

Let's examine what we just wrote. The callback function passed as the second parameter to `.attr()` runs on each of the visual elements selected (each of the `circle` elements in this case). During each execution of the callback, the return value of that callback function is then assigned to whatever aspect of the current element is being set (in this case the `cy` attribute).

The callback function takes two params:

- The individual `datum` object from the `runs` array that was attached to that particular visual element when we called `.data(runs)`
- The `index` of that `datum` in the`runs` array

In summary, what this does is loop through each `circle` in the SVG. For each `circle`, it looks at the `run` object attached to that `circle` and finds its `distance` property. It then feeds that data value into `yScale()`, which then converts it into its corresponding visual point. That visual point is then assigned to that circle's `cy` attribute. Since each data object has a different `distance` value, each `circle` is placed differently, vertically.

Creating a time scale

Let's position the circles horizontally, based on the date that their associated run happened. First, create a time scale. This is like a linear scale, but instead of mapping numeric values to visual points, it maps dates to visual points. Add the following to the bottom of app.js:

```
//scaleTime maps date values with numeric visual points
var xScale = d3.scaleTime();
xScale.range([0,WIDTH]);
xScale.domain([new Date('2017-10-1'), new Date('2017-10-31')]);
console.log(xScale(new Date('2017-10-28')));
console.log(xScale.invert(400));
```

Here's what our console should look like:

```
719.2145862552595
Sun Oct 15 2017 20:30:00 GMT-0700 (PDT)
>  |
```

You can now remove the two console.log() statements.

Parsing and formatting times

Note that the date properties of the objects in our runs array are strings and not date objects. This is a problem because xScale, as with all time scales, expects its data values to be date objects. Fortunately, D3 provides us an easy way to convert strings to dates and vice versa. We'll use a specially formatted string, based on the documentation (https://github.com/d3/d3-time-format#locale_format), to tell D3 how to parse the date string properties of the objects in our runs array into actual JavaScript date objects. Add the following at the end of app.js:

```
//this format matches our data in the runs array
var parseTime = d3.timeParse("%B%e, %Y at %-I:%M%p");
console.log(parseTime('October 3, 2017 at 6:00PM'));
var formatTime = d3.timeFormat("%B%e, %Y at %-I:%M%p");
//this format matches our data in the runs array
console.log(formatTime(new Date()));
```

Here's our Chrome console:

```
Tue Oct 03 2017 18:00:00 GMT-0700 (PDT)
May24, 2018 at 3:54PM
> |
```

Let's use this when calculating `cx` attributes for our circles. Remove the last two `console.log()` statements, and add the following to the bottom of `app.js`:

```
//use parseTime to convert the date string property on the datum object to
a Date object.
//xScale then converts this to a visual value
d3.selectAll('circle')
    .attr('cx', function(datum, index){
        return xScale(parseTime(datum.date));
    });
```

Here's what Chrome should look like:

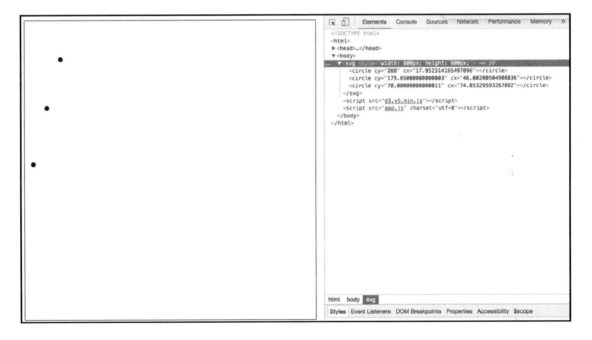

In summary, this selects all of the `circle` elements. It then sets the `cx` attribute of each `circle` to the result of a callback function. That callback function runs for each `circle` and takes the `run` data object associated with that `circle` and finds its `date` property (remember it's a string, for example, `'October 3, 2017 at 6:00PM'`). It passes that string value to `parseTime()` which then turns the string into an actual JavaScript date object. That date object is then passed to `xScale()`, which converts the date into a visual value. That visual value is then used for the `cx` attribute of whichever `circle` the callback function has just run on. Since each `date` property of the objects in the `runs` array is different, the `circles` have different horizontal locations.

Setting dynamic domains

At the moment, we're setting arbitrary min/max values for the domains of both distance and date. D3 can find the min/max of a dataset, so that our graph displays just the data ranges we need. All we need to do is pass the min/max methods a callback that gets called for each item of data in the `runs` array. D3 uses the callback to determine which properties of the datum object to compare for min/max.

Go to this part of the code:

```
var yScale = d3.scaleLinear(); //create the scale
yScale.range([HEIGHT, 0]); //set the visual range (for example 600 to 0)
yScale.domain([0, 10]); //set the data domain (for example 0 to 10)
```

Change it to this:

```
var yScale = d3.scaleLinear(); //create the scale
yScale.range([HEIGHT, 0]); //set the visual range (for example 600 to 0)
var yMin = d3.min(runs, function(datum, index){
    //compare distance properties of each item in the data array
    return datum.distance;
})
var yMax = d3.max(runs, function(datum, index){
    //compare distance properties of each item in the data array
    return datum.distance;
})
//now that I have the min/max of the data set for distance,
//we can use those values for the yScale domain
yScale.domain([yMin, yMax]);
console.log(yScale.domain());
```

Chrome should look as follows:

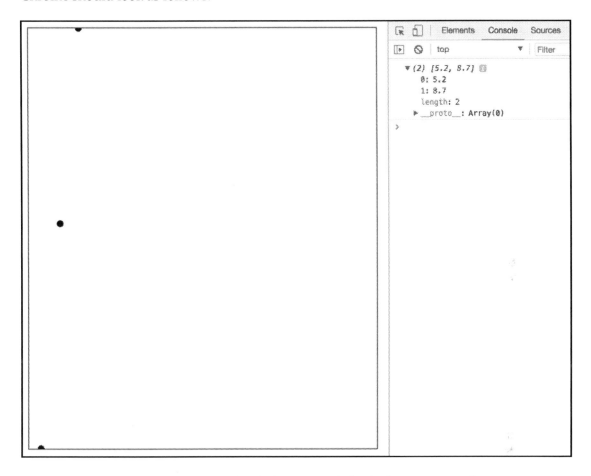

Let's examine what we just wrote. The following code finds the minimum distance:

```
var yMin = d3.min(runs, function(datum, index){
    //compare distance properties of each item in the data array
    return datum.distance;
})
```

D3 loops through the `runs` array (the first parameter) and calls the callback function (the second parameter) on each element of the array. The return value of that function is compared the return values of the callback function as it runs on the other elements. The lowest value is assigned to `yMin`. The same thing happens for `d3.max()` but with the highest value.

We can combine both the min/max functions into one `extent` function that returns an array that has the exact same structure as `[yMin, yMax]`. Let's look at the code we just wrote:

```
var yScale = d3.scaleLinear(); //create the scale
yScale.range([HEIGHT, 0]); //set the visual range (for example 600 to 0)
var yMin = d3.min(runs, function(datum, index){
    //compare distance properties of each item in the data array
    return datum.distance;
})
var yMax = d3.max(runs, function(datum, index){
    //compare distance properties of each item in the data array
    return datum.distance;
})
//now that we have the min/max of the data set for distance
//we can use those values for the yScale domain
yScale.domain([yMin, yMax]);
console.log(yScale.domain());
```

Change the previous code to this:

```
var yScale = d3.scaleLinear(); //create the scale
yScale.range([HEIGHT, 0]); //set the visual range (for example 600 to 0)
var yDomain = d3.extent(runs, function(datum, index){
    //compare distance properties of each item in the data array
    return datum.distance;
})
yScale.domain(yDomain);
```

It's much shorter, right? Let's do the same for the xScale's domain. Go to this part of the code:

```
//scaleTime maps date values with numeric visual points
var xScale = d3.scaleTime();
xScale.range([0,WIDTH]);
xScale.domain([new Date('2017-10-1'), new Date('2017-10-31')]);

//this format matches our data in the runs array
var parseTime = d3.timeParse("%B%e, %Y at %-I:%M%p");
//this format matches our data in the runs array
var formatTime = d3.timeFormat("%B%e, %Y at %-I:%M%p");
```

Change it to this:

```
var parseTime = d3.timeParse("%B%e, %Y at %-I:%M%p");
var formatTime = d3.timeFormat("%B%e, %Y at %-I:%M%p");
var xScale = d3.scaleTime();
xScale.range([0,WIDTH]);
```

```
var xDomain = d3.extent(runs, function(datum, index){
    return parseTime(datum.date);
});
xScale.domain(xDomain);
```

Notice we moved `parseTime` and `formatTime` up so they could be used within the `.extent()`. Here's what Chrome should look like:

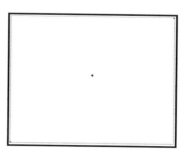

Dynamically generating SVG elements

Currently, we have just enough `<circle>` elements to fit our data. What if we don't want to count how many elements are in the array? D3 can create elements as needed. First, remove all `<circle>` elements from `index.html`. Your `<body>` tag should now look as follows:

```
<body>
    <svg></svg>
    <script src="https://d3js.org/d3.v5.min.js"></script>
    <script src="app.js" charset="utf-8"></script>
</body>
```

In `app.js`, go to this part of the code:

```
d3.selectAll('circle').data(runs)
    .attr('cy', function(datum, index){
        return yScale(datum.distance);
    });
```

Modify the code to create the circles:

```
//since no circles exist, we need to select('svg')
//so that d3 knows where to append the new circles
d3.select('svg').selectAll('circle')
    .data(runs) //attach the data as before
    //find the data objects that have not yet
```

```
        //been attached to visual elements
        .enter()
        //for each data object that hasn't been attached,
        //append a <circle> to the <svg>
        .append('circle');

    d3.selectAll('circle')
        .attr('cy', function(datum, index){
            return yScale(datum.distance);
        });
```

It should look exactly the same as before, but now circles are being created for each object in the runs array:

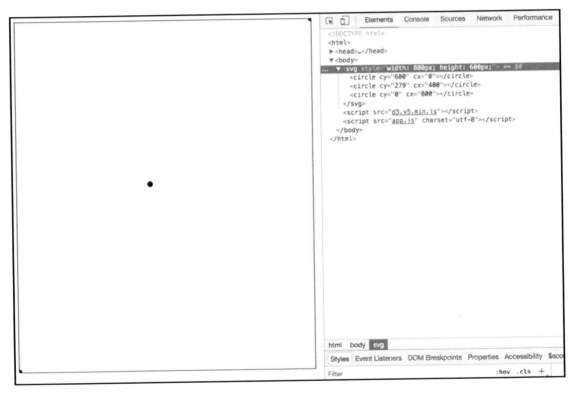

Here's a more in-depth explanation of what we just wrote. Take a look at the first line of the new code:

```
d3.select('svg').selectAll('circle')
```

This might seem unnecessary. Why not just do d3.selectAll('circle')? Well, at the moment, there are no circle elements. We're going to be appending circle elements dynamically, so d3.select('svg') tells D3 where to append them. We still need .selectAll('circle') though, so that when we call .data(runs) on the next line, D3 knows what elements to bind the various objects in the runs array to. But there aren't any circle elements to bind data to. That's OK..enter() finds the run objects that haven't been bound to any circle elements yet (in this case all of them). We then use .append('circle') to append a circle for each unbound run object that .enter() found.

Creating axes

D3 can automatically generate axes for you. Add the following to the bottom ofapp.js:

```
//pass the appropriate scale in as a parameter
var bottomAxis = d3.axisBottom(xScale);
```

This creates a bottom axis generator that can be used to insert an axis into any element you choose. Add the following code to the bottom of app.js to append a <g> element inside our SVG element and then insert a bottom axis inside it:

```
d3.select('svg')
    .append('g') //put everything inside a group
    .call(bottomAxis); //generate the axis within the group
```

Here's what Chrome should look like:

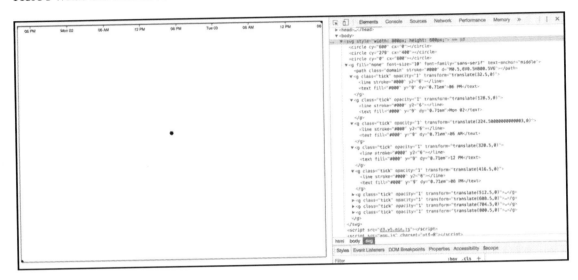

Display of Chrome

We want the axis to be at the bottom of the SVG, though. Modify the code we just wrote so it looks like this (note: we removed a; after `.call(bottomAxis)` and added `.attr('transform', 'translate(0,'+HEIGHT+')');`):

```
//pass the appropriate scale in as a parameter
var bottomAxis = d3.axisBottom(xScale);
d3.select('svg')
    .append('g') //put everything inside a group
    .call(bottomAxis) //generate the axis within the group
    //move it to the bottom
    .attr('transform', 'translate(0,'+HEIGHT+')');
```

Currently, our SVG clips the axis:

Let's alter our `svg` CSS so it doesn't clip any elements that extend beyond its bounds:

```
svg {
    overflow: visible;
}
```

Now it looks good:

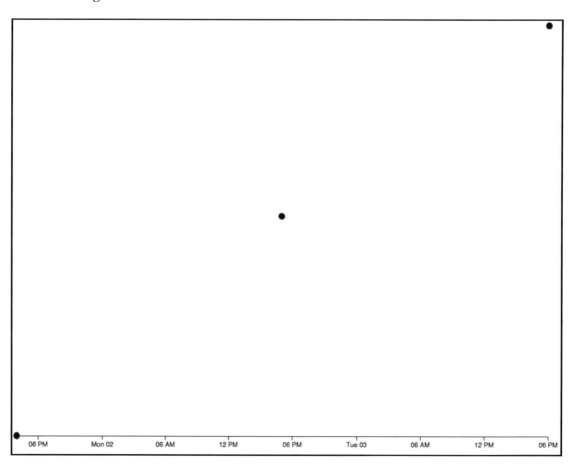

The left axis is pretty similar. Add the following to the bottom of app.js:

```
var leftAxis = d3.axisLeft(yScale);
d3.select('svg')
    .append('g')
    //no need to transform, since it's placed correctly initially
    .call(leftAxis);
```

Note: we don't need to set a `transform` attribute, since it starts out in the correct place initially:

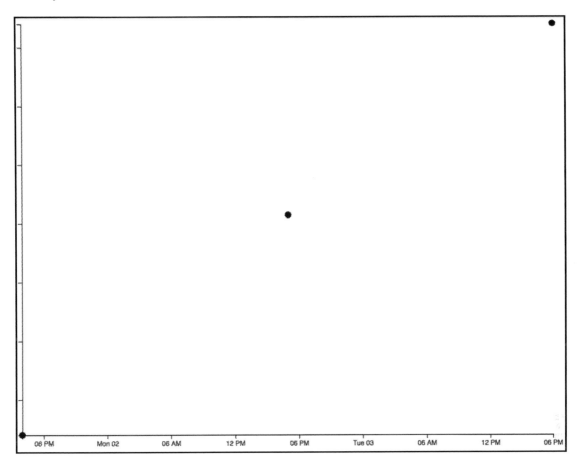

It's a little tough to see, so let's add the following at the bottom of `app.css`:

```
body {
    margin: 20px 40px;
}
```

Now our axes are complete:

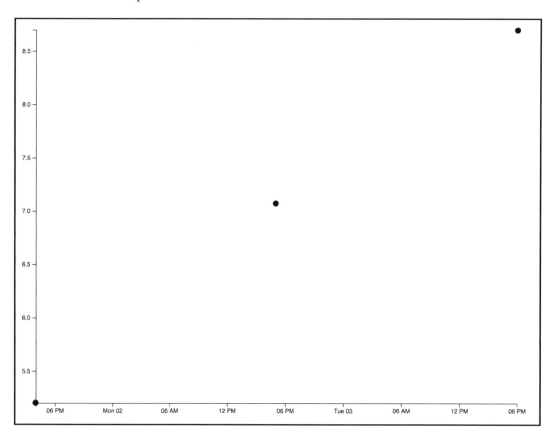

Displaying data in a table

Just for debugging purposes, let's create a table that will show all of our data. Make your
`<body>` tag in `index.html` look as follows:

```
<body>
    <svg></svg>
    <table>
        <thead>
            <tr>
                <th>id</th>
                <th>date</th>
                <th>distance</th>
            </tr>
```

```
        </thead>
        <tbody>
        </tbody>
    </table>
    <script src="https://d3js.org/d3.v5.min.js"></script>
    <script src="app.js" charset="utf-8"></script>
</body>
```

D3 can also be used to manipulate the DOM, just like jQuery. Let's populate the<tbody>in that style. Add the following to the bottom of app.js:

```
var createTable = function(){
    for (var i = 0; i < runs.length; i++) {
        var row = d3.select('tbody').append('tr');
        row.append('td').html(runs[i].id);
        row.append('td').html(runs[i].date);
        row.append('td').html(runs[i].distance);
    }
}

createTable();
```

Add some styling for the table at the bottom of app.css:

```
table, th, td {
    border: 1px solid black;
}
th, td {
    padding:10px;
    text-align: center;
}
```

Adjust the CSS for svg to add a bottom margin. This will create some space between the graph and the table:

```
svg {
    overflow: visible;
    margin-bottom: 50px;
}
```

Now the browser should look like this:

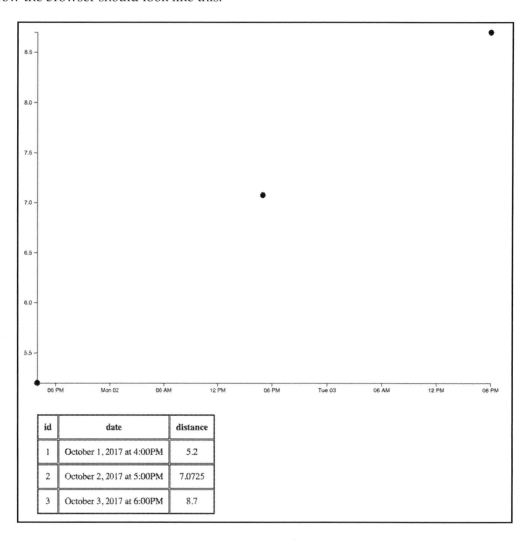

id	date	distance
1	October 1, 2017 at 4:00PM	5.2
2	October 2, 2017 at 5:00PM	7.0725
3	October 3, 2017 at 6:00PM	8.7

Summary

At this point, you have a static scatter plot and a table that displays its data. In Chapter 4, *Making a Basic Scatter Plot Interactive*, we will be learning how to make it interactive.

4
Making a Basic Scatter Plot Interactive

In the last chapter, we created a static scatter plot. In this chapter, we'll make it interactive so that we can add, update, and delete runs. You'll learn how to do the following:

- Create a click handler
- Remove data
- Drag an element
- Update data after a drag
- Create a zoom behavior that scales elements
- Update axes when zooming/panning
- Update click points after a transform
- Avoid redrawing the entire screen during rendering
- Hide elements beyond axes

The complete code for this section can be found here: https://github.com/ PacktPublishing/D3.js-Quick-Start-Guide/tree/master/Chapter04.

Creating a click handler

Let's say that we want it so that when the user clicks on the <svg> element, it creates a new run. Add the following to the bottom of app.js:

```
d3.select('svg').on('click', function(){
    //gets the x position of the mouse relative to the svg element
    var x = d3.event.offsetX;
    //gets the y position of the mouse relative to the svg element
    var y = d3.event.offsetY;
```

```
//get a date value from the visual point that we clicked on
var date = xScale.invert(x);
//get a numeric distance value from
//the visual point that we clicked on
var distance = yScale.invert(y);

//create a new "run" object
var newRun = {
    //generate a new id by adding 1 to the last run's id
    id: runs[runs.length-1].id+1,
    //format the date object created above to a string
    date: formatTime(date),
    distance: distance //add the distance
}
runs.push(newRun); //push the new run onto the runs array
createTable(); //render the table
});
```

Let's examine what we just wrote. Note that d3.select('svg').on('click', function(){ sets up a click handler on the svg element. The anonymous function that gets passed in as the second parameter to .on() gets called each time the user clicks on the SVG. Once inside that callback function, we use d3.event.offsetX to get the *x* position of the mouse inside the SVG, and we use d3.event.offsetY to get the *y* position. We then use xScale.invert() and yScale.invert() to turn the *x/y* visual points into data values (date and distance, respectively). We then use those data values to create a new run object. We create an ID for the new run by getting the ID of the last element in the runs array and adding 1 to it. Lastly, we push the new run on to the runs array and call createTable().

Click on the SVG to create a new run. You might notice that createTable() just adds on all the run rows again:

id	date	distance
1	October 1, 2017 at 4:00PM	5.2
2	October 2, 2017 at 5:00PM	7.0725
3	October 3, 2017 at 6:00PM	8.7
1	October 1, 2017 at 4:00PM	5.2
2	October 2, 2017 at 5:00PM	7.0725
3	October 3, 2017 at 6:00PM	8.7
4	October 3, 2017 at 3:15AM	7.5625

Let's alter the `createTable()` function so that when it runs, it clears out any rows previously created and re-renders everything. Add `d3.select('tbody').html('')` to the top of the `createTable` function in `app.js`:

```
var createTable = function(){
    //clear out all rows from the table
    d3.select('tbody').html('');
    for (var i = 0; i < runs.length; i++) {
        var row = d3.select('tbody').append('tr');
        row.append('td').html(runs[i].id);
        row.append('td').html(runs[i].date);
        row.append('td').html(runs[i].distance);
    }
}
```

Now refresh the page and click on the SVG to create a new run. The table should then look like this:

id	date	distance
1	October 1, 2017 at 4:00PM	5.2
2	October 2, 2017 at 5:00PM	7.0725
3	October 3, 2017 at 6:00PM	8.7
4	October 3, 2017 at 4:22AM	7.352499999999999

The only issue now is that circles aren't being created when you click on the SVG. To fix this, let's wrap the code for creating <circle> elements in a render function, and call render() immediately after it's defined:

```
var render = function(){

    var yScale = d3.scaleLinear();
    yScale.range([HEIGHT, 0]);
    yDomain = d3.extent(runs, function(datum, index){
        return datum.distance;
    })
    yScale.domain(yDomain);

    d3.select('svg').selectAll('circle')
        .data(runs)
        .enter()
        .append('circle');

    d3.selectAll('circle')
        .attr('cy', function(datum, index){
            return yScale(datum.distance);
        });

    var parseTime = d3.timeParse("%B%e, %Y at %-I:%M%p");
    var formatTime = d3.timeFormat("%B%e, %Y at %-I:%M%p");
    var xScale = d3.scaleTime();
    xScale.range([0,WIDTH]);
    xDomain = d3.extent(runs, function(datum, index){
        return parseTime(datum.date);
    });
    xScale.domain(xDomain);
```

```
    d3.selectAll('circle')
        .attr('cx', function(datum, index){
            return xScale(parseTime(datum.date));
        });

}
render();
```

If you refresh the browser, you'll see an error in the console. This is because `bottomAxis` and `leftAxis` use `xScale` and `yScale` that are now scoped to exist only inside the `render()` function. For future use, let's move `xScale` and `yScale` out of the render function along with the code for creating the domains/ranges:

```
var parseTime = d3.timeParse("%B%e, %Y at %-I:%M%p");
var formatTime = d3.timeFormat("%B%e, %Y at %-I:%M%p");
var xScale = d3.scaleTime();
xScale.range([0,WIDTH]);
xDomain = d3.extent(runs, function(datum, index){
    return parseTime(datum.date);
});
xScale.domain(xDomain);

var yScale = d3.scaleLinear();
yScale.range([HEIGHT, 0]);
yDomain = d3.extent(runs, function(datum, index){
    return datum.distance;
})
yScale.domain(yDomain);
var render = function(){

    //since no circles exist,
    //we need to select('svg') so that
    //d3 knows where to append the new circles
    d3.select('svg').selectAll('circle')
        //attach the data as before
        .data(runs)
        //find the data objects that have not yet
        //been attached to visual elements
        .enter()
        //for each data object that hasn't been attached,
        //append a <circle> to the <svg>
        .append('circle');
```

```
        d3.selectAll('circle')
            .attr('cy', function(datum, index){
                return yScale(datum.distance);
            });

        d3.selectAll('circle')
            .attr('cx', function(datum, index){
                //use parseTime to convert
                //the date string property on the datum object
                //to a Date object,
                //which xScale then converts to a visual value
                return xScale(parseTime(datum.date));
            });

    }
    render();
```

Now go to the bottom of `app.js` and add a line to call `render()` inside our `<svg>` click handler:

```
var newRun = {
    id: runs[runs.length-1].id+1,
    date: formatTime(date),
    distance: distance
}
runs.push(newRun);
createTable();
render(); //add this line
```

Now when you click the SVG, a circle will appear:

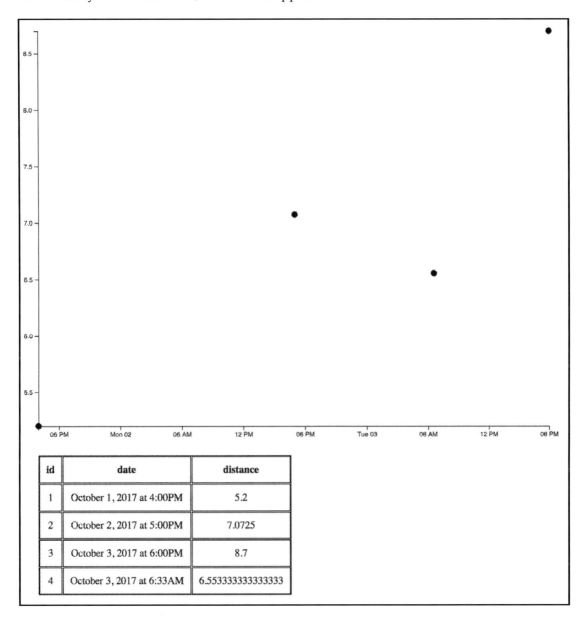

id	date	distance
1	October 1, 2017 at 4:00PM	5.2
2	October 2, 2017 at 5:00PM	7.0725
3	October 3, 2017 at 6:00PM	8.7
4	October 3, 2017 at 6:33AM	6.553333333333333

Removing data

Let's set up a click handler on all `<circle>` elements so that when the user clicks on `<circle>`, D3 will remove that circle and its associated data element from the array. Add the following code at the bottom of the `render` function declaration we wrote in the last section. We do this so that the click handlers are attached *after* the circles are created:

```
//put this at the bottom of the render function,
//so that click handlers are attached when the circle is created
d3.selectAll('circle').on('click', function(datum, index){
    //stop click event from propagating to
    //the SVG element and creating a run
    d3.event.stopPropagation();
    //create a new array that has removed the run
    //with the correct id. Set it to the runs var
    runs = runs.filter(function(run, index){
        return run.id != datum.id;
    });
    render(); //re-render dots
    createTable(); //re-render table
});
```

Let's examine the previous code. The first line selects all `<circle>` elements and creates a click handler on each of them. However, `d3.event.stopPropagation();` prevents the click from bubbling up the DOM to the SVG. If we don't add it, the click handler on the SVG will fire as well, when we click on a circle. This would create an additional run every time we try to remove a run. Next, we call the following:

```
runs = runs.filter(function(run, index){
 return run.id != datum.id;
});
```

This loops through the `runs` array and filters out any objects that have an `id` property that matches the `id` property of `datum` that is associated with `<circle>` that was clicked. Notice that the callback function in `.on('click', function(datum, index){` takes two parameters: `datum`, the run object associated with that `<circle>`, and the `index` of the run object in the `runs` array.

Once we've filtered out the correct run object from the `runs` array, we call `render()` and `createdTable()` to re-render the graph and the table.

But if we click on the middle circle and examine the **Elements** tab of the Developer Tools, we'll see that the `<circle>` element hasn't been removed:

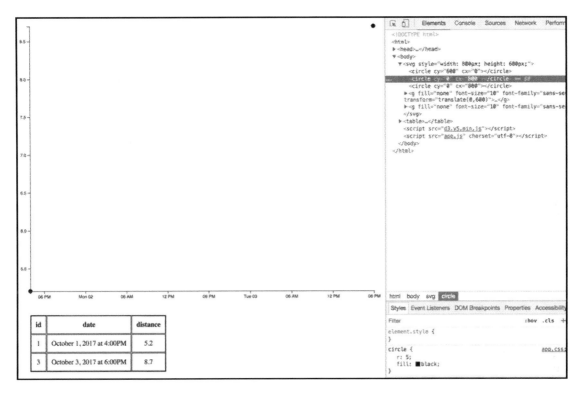

Elements tab showing the <circle> element

In the previous screenshot, it appears as though there are only two circles, but really the middle one has had its cx set to 800 and its cy set to 0. It's overlapping the other circle in the same position. This is because we've removed the second element in the runs array. When we re-render the graph, the runs array only has two objects; the second run object used to be the third run object before we removed the middle run. Now that it's the second run object, the second <circle> is assigned its data. The third circle still has its old data assigned to it, so both the second and the third circle have the same data and are therefore placed in the same location.

Let's put the circles in <g> so that it's easy to clear out all the circles and re-render them when we remove a run. This way we won't have any extra <circle> elements lying around when we try to remove them. This approach is similar to what we do when re-rendering the table. Adjust your <svg> element in index.html so it looks as follows:

```
<svg>
    <g id="points"></g>
</svg>
```

Now we can clear out the <circle> elements each time render() is called. This is a little crude, but it'll work for now. Later on, we'll do things in a more elegant fashion. At the top of the render() function declaration, add d3.select('#points').html(''); and adjust the next line from d3.select('svg').selectAll('circle') to d3.select('#points').selectAll('circle'):

```
//adjust the code at the top of your render function
 //clear out all circles when rendering d3.select('#points').html('');
 //add circles to #points group, not svg
d3.select('#points').selectAll('circle') .data(runs) .enter()
.append('circle');
```

Now if we click on the middle circle, the element is removed from the DOM:

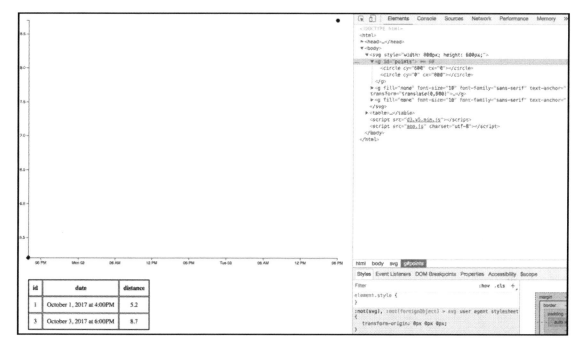

Removing the element from the DOM

If you try to delete all the circles and then add a new one, you'll get an error:

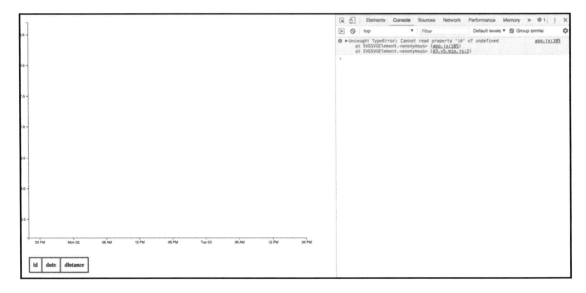

Displaying the error you get when deleting all the circles and adding a new one

This is because our code for creating `newRun` in the SVG click handler needs some work:

```
var newRun = { //create a new "run" object
    //generate a new id by adding 1 to the last run's id
    id: runs[runs.length-1].id+1,
    //format the date object created above to a string
    date: formatTime(date),
    distance: distance //add the distance
}
```

This is because when there are no run elements in the `runs` array, `runs[runs.length-1]` tries to access an element at index −1 in the array. Inside the `<svg>` click handler, let's put in a little code to handle when the user has deleted all runs and tries to add a new one:

```
//inside svg click handler
var newRun = {
    //add this line
    id: ( runs.length > 0 ) ? runs[runs.length-1].id+1 : 1,
    date: formatTime(date),
    distance: distance
}
```

Here's what Chrome should look like now if you delete all the runs and then try to add a new one:

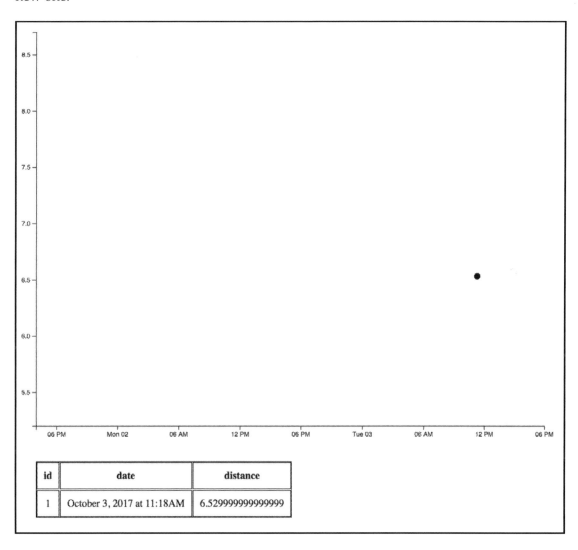

id	date	distance
1	October 3, 2017 at 11:18AM	6.529999999999999

Lastly, let's put in some CSS, so we know we're clicking on a circle. First, add `transition: r 0.5s linear, fill 0.5s linear;` to the CSS code you've already written for `circle`:

```
circle {
    r: 5;
    fill: black;
```

```
        /* add this transition to original code */
        transition: r 0.5s linear,  fill 0.5s linear;
}
```

Then add this to the bottom of `app.css`:

```
/* add this css for the hover state */
circle:hover {
    r:10;
    fill: blue;
}
```

Here's what a circle should look like when you hover over it:

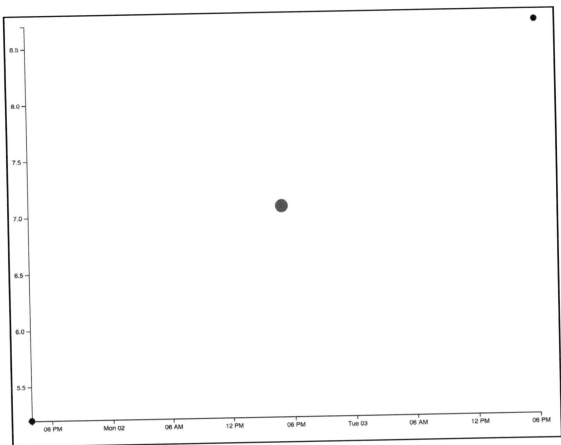

Dragging an element

We want to be able to update the data for a run by dragging the associated circle. To do this, we'll use a behavior, which you can think of as a combination of multiple event handlers. For a drag behavior, there are three callbacks:

- When the user starts to drag
- Each time the user moves the cursor before releasing the *mouse* button
- When the user releases the *mouse* button

There are two steps whenever we create a behavior:

1. Create the behavior
2. Attach the behavior to one or more elements

Put the following code at the bottom of the render() function declaration:

```
//put this code at the end of the render function
var drag = function(datum) {
    var x = d3.event.x;
    var y = d3.event.y;
    d3.select(this).attr('cx', x);
    d3.select(this).attr('cy', y);
}
var dragBehavior = d3.drag()
    .on('drag', drag);
d3.selectAll('circle').call(dragBehavior);
```

You can now drag the circles around, but the data doesn't update:

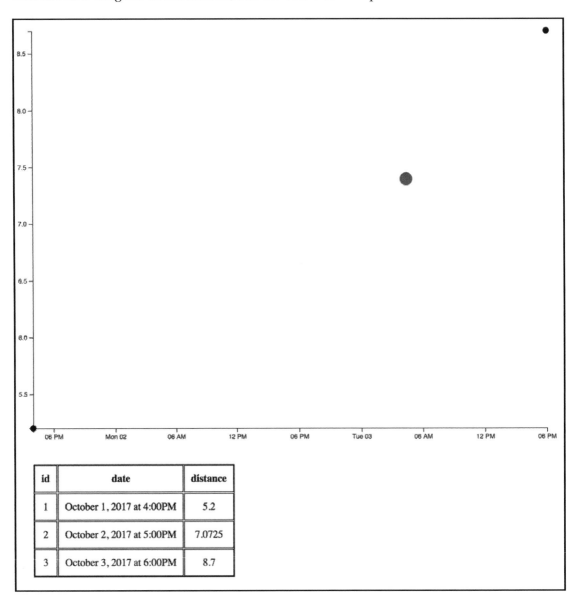

id	date	distance
1	October 1, 2017 at 4:00PM	5.2
2	October 2, 2017 at 5:00PM	7.0725
3	October 3, 2017 at 6:00PM	8.7

Let's examine how this code works:

```
var drag = function(datum){
  var x = d3.event.x;
  var y = d3.event.y;
```

```
d3.select(this).attr('cx', x);
d3.select(this).attr('cy', y);
}
```

This `drag` function will be used as a callback anytime the user moves the cursor before releasing the mouse button. It gets the *x* and *y* coordinates of the mouse and sets the `cx` and `cy` values of the element being dragged (`d3.select(this)`) to those coordinates.

Next, we generate a drag behavior that will, at the appropriate time, call the `drag` function that was just explained:

```
var dragBehavior = d3.drag()
  .on('drag', drag);
```

Lastly, we attach that behavior to all the `<circle>` elements:

```
d3.selectAll('circle').call(dragBehavior);
```

Updating data after a drag

Now we're going to add functionality so that when the user releases the mouse button, the data for the run object associated with the circle being dragged gets updated.

First, let's create the callback function that will get called when the user releases the mouse button. Toward the bottom of the `render()` function declaration, add the following code just above `var drag = function(datum){`:

```
var dragEnd = function(datum){
    var x = d3.event.x;
    var y = d3.event.y;

    var date = xScale.invert(x);
    var distance = yScale.invert(y);
    datum.date = formatTime(date);
    datum.distance = distance;
    createTable();
}
```

Now attach that function to `dragBehavior` so that it is called when the user stops dragging a circle. Look at the following code:

```
var dragBehavior = d3.drag()
    .on('drag', drag);
```

Change it to this:

```
var dragBehavior = d3.drag()
    .on('drag', drag)
    .on('end', dragEnd);
```

Now, once you stop dragging a circle around, you should see the data in the table change:

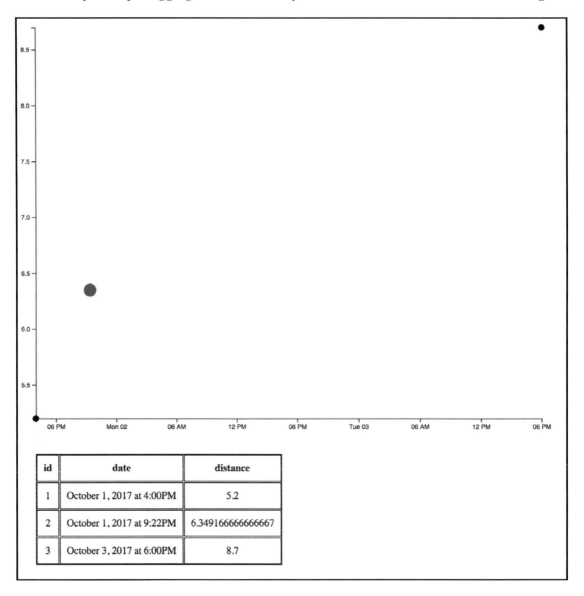

id	date	distance
1	October 1, 2017 at 4:00PM	5.2
2	October 1, 2017 at 9:22PM	6.349166666666667
3	October 3, 2017 at 6:00PM	8.7

Let's change the color of a circle while it's being dragged too. Add this to the bottom of `app.css`:

```
circle:active {
    fill: red;
}
```

When you drag a circle, it should turn red.

Creating a zoom behavior that scales elements

Another behavior we can create is the zooming/panning ability. Once this functionality is complete, you will be able to zoom in and out on different parts of the graph by doing one of the following:

- A two-finger drag on a trackpad
- Rotating your mouse wheel
- Pinching/spreading on a trackpad

You will also be able to pan left, right, up, and down on the graph by clicking and dragging on the SVG element.

Put the following code at the bottom of `app.js`:

```
var zoomCallback = function(){
    d3.select('#points').attr("transform", d3.event.transform);
}
```

This is the callback function that will be called when the user attempts to zoom or pan. All it does is take the zoom or pan action and turn it into a `transform` attribute that gets applied to the `<g id="points"></g>` element that contains the circles. Now add the following code to the bottom of `app.js` to create the `zoom` behavior and attach it to the `svg` element:

```
var zoom = d3.zoom()
    .on('zoom', zoomCallback);
d3.select('svg').call(zoom);
```

Now, if we zoom out, the graph should look something like this:

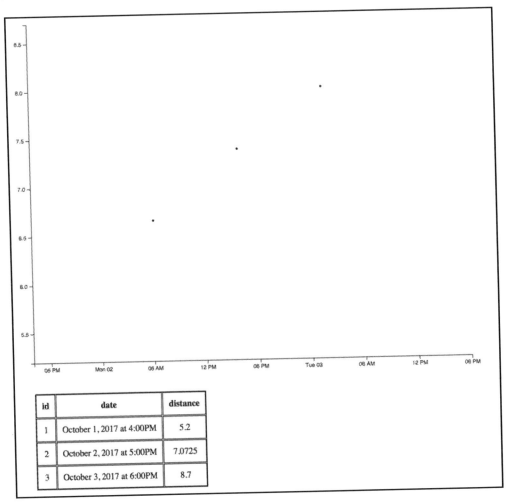

id	date	distance
1	October 1, 2017 at 4:00PM	5.2
2	October 2, 2017 at 5:00PM	7.0725
3	October 3, 2017 at 6:00PM	8.7

Updating axes when zooming and panning

Now when we zoom, the points move in/out. When we pan, they move vertically/horizontally. Unfortunately, the axes don't update accordingly. Let's first add IDs to the <g> elements that contain them. Find the following code:

```
var bottomAxis = d3.axisBottom(xScale);
d3.select('svg')
```

```
    .append('g')
    .call(bottomAxis)
    .attr('transform', 'translate(0,'+HEIGHT+')');
var leftAxis = d3.axisLeft(yScale);
d3.select('svg')
    .append('g')
    .call(leftAxis);
```

Add .attr('id', 'x-axis') after the first .append('g'), and .attr('id', 'y-axis') after the second .append('g'):

```
d3.select('svg')
    .append('g')
    .attr('id', 'x-axis') //add an id
    .call(bottomAxis)
    .attr('transform', 'translate(0,'+HEIGHT+')');
var leftAxis = d3.axisLeft(yScale);
d3.select('svg')
    .append('g')
    .attr('id', 'y-axis') //add an id
    .call(leftAxis);
```

Now let's use those IDs to adjust the axes when we zoom. Find this code:

```
var zoomCallback = function(){
    d3.select('#points').attr("transform", d3.event.transform);
}
```

Add the following to the end of the function declaration:

```
d3.select('#x-axis')
    .call(bottomAxis.scale(d3.event.transform.rescaleX(xScale)));
d3.select('#y-axis')
    .call(leftAxis.scale(d3.event.transform.rescaleY(yScale)));
```

Now zoomCallback should look as follows:

```
var zoomCallback = function(){
    d3.select('#points').attr("transform", d3.event.transform);
    d3.select('#x-axis')
      .call(bottomAxis.scale(d3.event.transform.rescaleX(xScale)));
    d3.select('#y-axis')
      .call(leftAxis.scale(d3.event.transform.rescaleY(yScale)));
}
```

There are two things to note about the previous code:

- `bottomAxis.scale()` tells the axis to redraw itself.
- `d3.event.transform.rescaleX(xScale)` returns a value indicating how the bottom axis should rescale.

Now when you zoom out, the axes should redraw themselves:

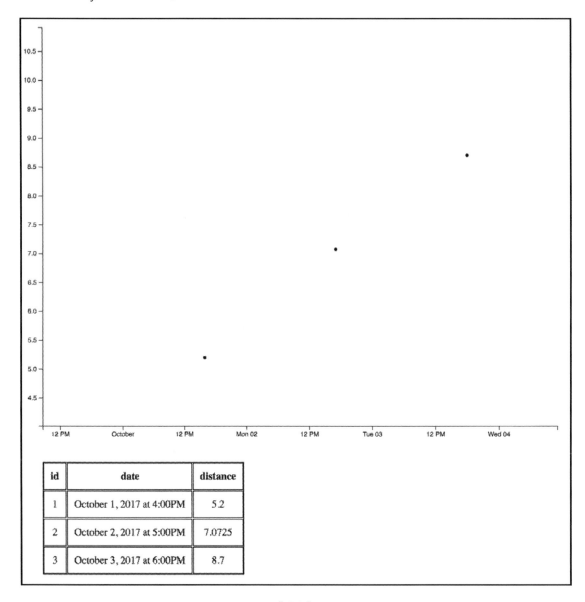

Updating click points after a transform

Try zooming and panning and then clicking on the SVG to create a new run. You'll notice it's in the wrong place. That's because the SVG click handler has no idea that a zoom or pan has happened. Currently, if you click on the visual point, no matter how much you may have zoomed or panned, the click handler still converts it as if you had never zoomed or panned.

When we zoom, we need to save the transformation information to a variable so that we can use it later to figure out how to properly create circles and runs. Find the `zoomCallback` declaration and add `var lastTransform = null` right before it. Then add `lastTransform = d3.event.transform;` to the beginning of the function declaration. It should look as follows:

```
var lastTransform = null; //add this
var zoomCallback = function(){
    lastTransform = d3.event.transform; //add this
    d3.select('#points').attr("transform", d3.event.transform);
    d3.select('#x-axis')
      .call(bottomAxis.scale(d3.event.transform.rescaleX(xScale)));
    d3.select('#y-axis')
      .call(leftAxis.scale(d3.event.transform.rescaleY(yScale)));
}
```

Now whenever the user zooms or pans the transformation data that was used to shrink or move the SVG and axes is saved in the `lastTransform` variable. Use that variable when clicking on the SVG.

Find these two lines at the beginning of the SVG click handler:

```
var x = d3.event.offsetX;
var y = d3.event.offsetY;
```

Change them to the following:

```
var x = lastTransform.invertX(d3.event.offsetX);
var y = lastTransform.invertY(d3.event.offsetY);
```

Your click handler should look like this now:

```
d3.select('svg').on('click', function(){
    var x = lastTransform.invertX(d3.event.offsetX); //adjust this
    var y = lastTransform.invertY(d3.event.offsetY); //adjust this

    var date = xScale.invert(x);
    var distance = yScale.invert(y);
```

```
        var newRun = {
            id: ( runs.length > 0 ) ? runs[runs.length-1].id+1 : 1,
            date: formatTime(date),
            distance: distance
        }
        runs.push(newRun);
        createTable();
        render();
    });
```

But now click before any zoom is broken, since `lastTransform` will be null:

Find the code that we just wrote for the SVG click handler:

```
        var x = lastTransform.invertX(d3.event.offsetX);
        var y = lastTransform.invertY(d3.event.offsetY);
```

Adjust it so it looks as follows:

```
        var x = d3.event.offsetX;
        var y = d3.event.offsetY;

        if(lastTransform !== null){
            x = lastTransform.invertX(d3.event.offsetX);
            y = lastTransform.invertY(d3.event.offsetY);
        }
```

Now initially, x and y are set to d3.event.offsetX and d3.event.offsetY, respectively. If a zoom or pan occurs, lastTransform will not be null, so we overwrite x and y with the transformed values.

Add a new run initially:

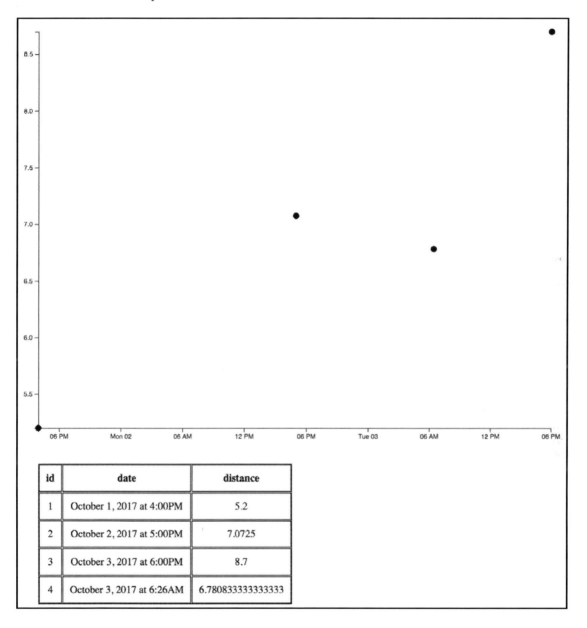

id	date	distance
1	October 1, 2017 at 4:00PM	5.2
2	October 2, 2017 at 5:00PM	7.0725
3	October 3, 2017 at 6:00PM	8.7
4	October 3, 2017 at 6:26AM	6.780833333333333

Now pan right and add a new point:

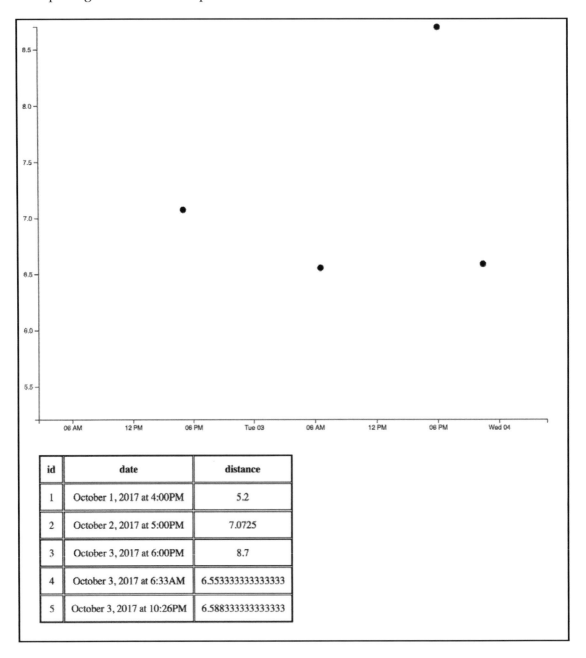

id	date	distance
1	October 1, 2017 at 4:00PM	5.2
2	October 2, 2017 at 5:00PM	7.0725
3	October 3, 2017 at 6:00PM	8.7
4	October 3, 2017 at 6:33AM	6.553333333333333
5	October 3, 2017 at 10:26PM	6.588333333333333

Avoiding redrawing the entire screen during rendering

At the moment, every time we call `render()`, we wipe all `<circle>` elements from `<svg>`. This is inefficient. Let's just remove the ones we don't want

At the top of the `render()` function, assign `d3.select('#points').selectAll('circle').data(runs)` to a variable, so we can use it later. This helps preserve how DOM elements are assigned to data elements in the next sections. Find this at the top of the `render()` function declaration:

```
d3.select('#points').html('');
d3.select('#points').selectAll('circle')
  .data(runs)
  .enter()
  .append('circle');
```

Change it to this:

```
d3.select('#points').html('');
var circles = d3.select('#points')
  .selectAll('circle')
  .data(runs);
circles.enter().append('circle');
```

Next, remove the `d3.select('#points').html('');` line. We'll use `.exit()` to find the selection of circles that haven't been matched with data, and then we'll use `.remove()` to remove those circles. Add the following after the last line we just wrote (`circles.enter().append('circle');`):

```
circles.exit().remove();
```

Reload the page, click on the center (second) circle. You'll notice it looks as if the circle disappears, and the circle in the upper-right briefly gains a hover state and then shrinks back down. That's not really what's happening.

If we click on the middle circle (second), it deletes the second run object in the `runs` array, and the third run object moves down to replace it in second place. We now only have an array of two run objects: the first and what used to be the third (but is now the second). When `render()` gets called again, what was the middle (second) circle gets assigned to what used to be the third run object in the `runs` array (but is now the second). This "run" object used to be assigned to the third circle, which was in the upper right. But now, since there are only two runs, that third (upper-right) circle gets deleted when we call `circles.exit().remove();`. The second circle's data has changed now, and it jumps to the upper–right corner to match that data. It used to have a hover state, but all of a sudden it's moved out from under the cursor, so it shrinks back down to normal size and becomes black.

To avoid these effects, we need to make sure that each circle stays with the data it used to be assigned to when we call `render()`. To do this, we can tell D3 to map `<circles>` to datum by ID, rather than index, in the array. At the top of the `render()` function, find this code:

```
var circles = d3.select('#points')
  .selectAll('circle')
  .data(runs);
```

Change it to this:

```
var circles = d3.select('#points')
  .selectAll('circle')
  .data(runs, function(datum){
  return datum.id
});
```

This tells D3 to use the `id` property of each run object when determining which `<circle>` element to assign the data object to. It basically assigns that `id` property of the run object to the `<circle>` element initially. That way, when the second run object is deleted, `circles.exit().remove();` will find the circle that had the corresponding ID (the middle circle) and remove it.

Now clicking on the middle circle should work correctly.

Hiding elements beyond an axis

If you pan or zoom extensively, you'll notice that the circles are visible beyond the bounds of the axes:

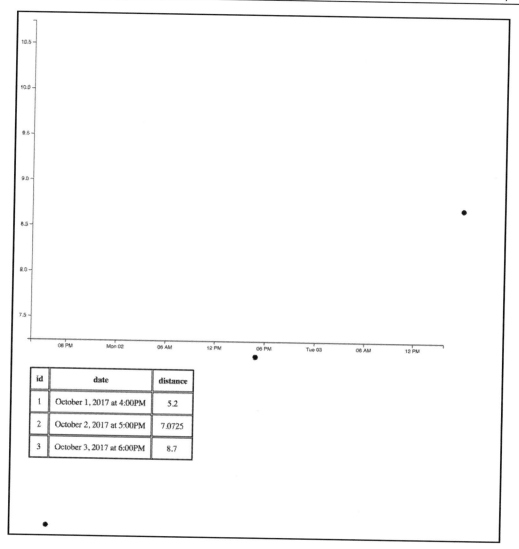

id	date	distance
1	October 1, 2017 at 4:00PM	5.2
2	October 2, 2017 at 5:00PM	7.0725
3	October 3, 2017 at 6:00PM	8.7

To hide elements once they get beyond an axis, we can just add an outer SVG with id="container" around our current <svg> element in index.html:

```
<svg id="container">
    <svg>
        <g id="points"></g>
    </svg>
</svg>
```

Now replace all d3.select('svg') code with d3.select('#container'). You can perform a find-and-replace. There should be five instances to change:

```
d3.select('#container')
    .style('width', WIDTH)
    .style('height', HEIGHT);

//
// lots of code omitted here, including render() declaration...
//

var bottomAxis = d3.axisBottom(xScale);
d3.select('#container')
    .append('g')
    .attr('id', 'x-axis')
    .call(bottomAxis)
    .attr('transform', 'translate(0,'+HEIGHT+')');

var leftAxis = d3.axisLeft(yScale);
d3.select('#container')
    .append('g')
    .attr('id', 'y-axis')
    .call(leftAxis);

//
// code for create table omitted here...
//

d3.select('#container').on('click', function(){
    //
    // click handler functionality omitted
    //
});

//
// zoomCallback code omitted here
//

var zoom = d3.zoom()
    .on('zoom', zoomCallback);
d3.select('#container').call(zoom);
```

And, lastly, adjust CSS to replace `svg {` with `#container {`:

```
#container {
    overflow: visible;
    margin-bottom: 50px;
}
```

Now circles should be hidden once they move beyond the bounds of the inner `<svg>` element:

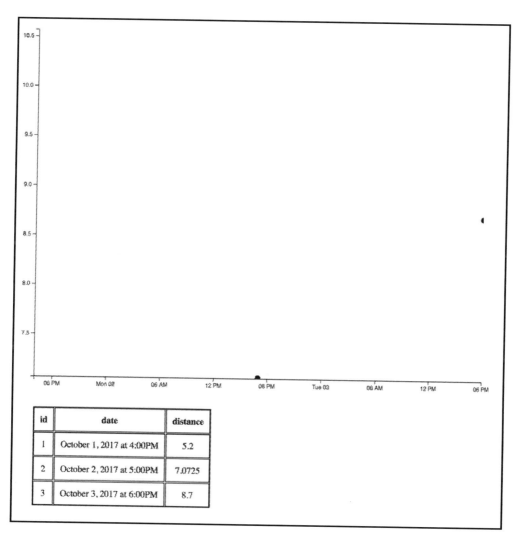

Summary

In this chapter, we've learned the basics of D3 and have created a fully interactive scatter plot. In the next chapter, we'll learn how to use AJAX to make an asynchronous request that will populate a bar graph.

5
Creating a Bar Graph Using a Data File

AJAX stands for **Asynchronous JavaScript And XML**. Basically, what we can do is use JavaScript to load data into the page after it has loaded. This is a great way to generate a graph based on user interaction. In this chapter, we'll use AJAX to build a bar graph. By the end of the chapter, you should be able to do the following:

- Use AJAX to make an asynchronous call to an external data file
- Create a bar graph

The complete code for this section can be found here: `https://github.com/PacktPublishing/D3.js-Quick-Start-Guide/tree/master/Chapter05`.

Setting up our application

Let's create our standard setup in `index.html`:

```
<!DOCTYPE html>
<html lang="en" dir="ltr">
    <head>
        <link rel="stylesheet" href="app.css">
    </head>
    <body>
        <svg></svg>
        <script src="https://d3js.org/d3.v5.min.js"></script>
        <script src="app.js" charset="utf-8"></script>
    </body>
</html>
```

Now add the following code to `app.js`:

```
var WIDTH = 800;
var HEIGHT = 600;

d3.select('svg')
    .style('width', WIDTH)
    .style('height', HEIGHT);
```

Now add the following code to `app.css`:

```
svg {
    border:1px solid black;
}
```

This is what we should have:

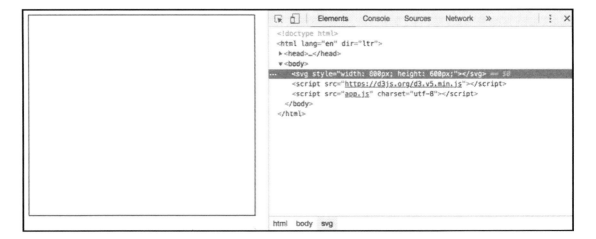

Creating an external file to hold our data

Let's create a `data.json` file, which will hold fake data regarding how often job posts require certain skills. This should be the contents of the file:

```
[
  {
    "name": "HTML",
    "count": 21
  },
  {
    "name": "CSS",
```

```
    "count": 17
  },
  {
    "name": "Responsive Web Design",
    "count": 17
  },
  {
    "name": "JavaScript",
    "count": 17
  },
  {
    "name": "Git",
    "count": 16
  },
  {
    "name": "Angular.js",
    "count": 9
  },
  {
    "name": "Node.js",
    "count": 9
  },
  {
    "name": "PostgreSQL",
    "count": 8
  },
  {
    "name": "Agile Project Management",
    "count": 8
  },
  {
    "name": "MongoDB",
    "count": 7
  },
  {
    "name": "Trello",
    "count": 7
  },
  {
    "name": "Testing / TDD",
    "count": 7
  },
  {
    "name": "jQuery",
    "count": 7
  },
  {
    "name": "User Testing",
```

```
    "count": 6
  },
  {
    "name": "MySQL",
    "count": 6
  },
  {
    "name": "PHP",
    "count": 6
  },
  {
    "name": "React.js",
    "count": 6
  },
  {
    "name": "AJAX",
    "count": 6
  },
  {
    "name": "Express.js",
    "count": 5
  },
  {
    "name": "Heroku",
    "count": 5
  },
  {
    "name": "Wireframing",
    "count": 5
  },
  {
    "name": "Sass/SCSS",
    "count": 5
  },
  {
    "name": "Mobile Web",
    "count": 4
  },
  {
    "name": "Rails",
    "count": 4
  },
  {
    "name": "WordPress",
    "count": 4
  },
  {
    "name": "Drupal",
```

```
      "count": 3
    },
    {
      "name": "Ruby",
      "count": 3
    },
    {
      "name": "Ember.js",
      "count": 3
    },
    {
      "name": "Python",
      "count": 3
    },
    {
      "name": "Amazon EC2",
      "count": 2
    },
    {
      "name": "Computer Science degree",
      "count": 1
    },
    {
      "name": "Backbone.js",
      "count": 1
    },
    {
      "name": "Less",
      "count": 1
    },
    {
      "name": "Prototyping",
      "count": 1
    },
    {
      "name": "Redis",
      "count": 1
    }
  ]
```

Making an AJAX request

Now we're going to use JavaScript to make a request for some data.

Writing the basic code

D3 has lots of different methods for making AJAX requests to files of different data types:

```
d3.json('path').then(function(data){
    //do something with the json data here
});
d3.csv('path').then(function(data){
    //do something with the csv data here
});
d3.tsv('path').then(function(data){
    //do something with the tsv data here
});
d3.xml('path').then(function(data){
    //do something with the xml data here
});
d3.html('path').then(function(data){
    //do something with the html data here
});
d3.text('path').then(function(data){
    //do something with the text data here
});
```

Since our data is in JSON format, we'll use the first kind of call. Add the following to the end of `app.js`:

```
d3.json('data.json').then(function(data){ console.log(data); });
```

Handling file access

If you opened the `index.html` file in Chrome directly, instead of serving it on a web server, you'll notice we've encountered an error. Check your developer console:

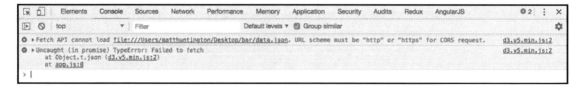

The issue here is that web browsers are not supposed to make AJAX requests to files on your computer. If they could, this would be a huge security flaw because any website could access files on your computer. Let's create a basic file server. To do this, you'll need to `installNode.js` (`https://nodejs.org/en/`). Once that's done, open your computer's Terminal:

- For Mac: command + *Space*, and then type `terminal` and hit Ent*er*.
- For Windows: click **Start**, type `cmd`,and hit *Enter*.

Next, type the following into your Terminal:

```
npm install -g http-server
```

If you get error messages, try this:

```
sudo npm install -g http-server
```

This installs a basic `http-server` that was built using `Node.js`. To run it, use the Terminal to navigate to the directory where you saved your code (type `cd` to change folders in the Terminal) and run the following:

```
http-server .
```

You should see something such as this:

```
Matts-MacBook-Pro-2:bar matthuntington$ http-server .
Starting up http-server, serving .
Available on:
  http://127.0.0.1:8080
  http://10.0.0.45:8080
Hit CTRL-C to stop the server
```

Now go to `http://localhost:8080/` in your browser. You should now see that your AJAX call is succeeding (if you have issues, hold down shift and hit the refresh button to force the browser to reload all files that may have been cached):

Using AJAX data to create SVG elements

Now that our AJAX calls are succeeding, let's start building our app. From here on out, it's all basic JavaScript and D3. Note that everything we'll write for the rest of this lesson is done within the success callback of our AJAX request. In production, we might want to move this code elsewhere, but for now this is easier for learning. Let's create some rectangles for our bar graph. The bottom of `app.js` (the callback to the AJAX request) should now look as follows:

```
d3.json('data.json').then(function(data){
    d3.select('svg').selectAll('rect')
        .data(data)
        .enter()
        .append('rect');
});
```

Our **Elements** tab in our dev tools should look something like this:

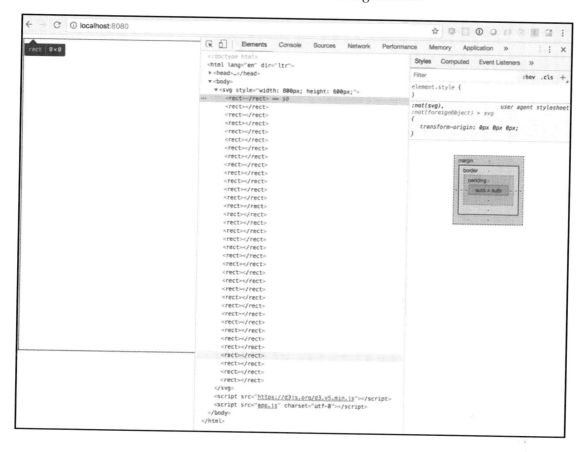

Adjusting the height and the width of the bars

Let's create a scale that maps the count property of each element in data to a visual height for the corresponding bar. We'll use a linear scale. Remember to map HEIGHT of the graph to a very low data point and the top of the graph (0 in the range) map to a very high data value. Add this code to the bottom of the AJAX callback:

```
var yScale = d3.scaleLinear();
yScale.range([HEIGHT, 0]);
var yMin = d3.min(data, function(datum, index){
    return datum.count;
})
var yMax = d3.max(data, function(datum, index){
    return datum.count;
})
yScale.domain([yMin, yMax]);
```

We could use d3.extent, but we're going to need the individual min values later on. Immediately after the previous code, let's tell D3 to adjust the height of the rectangles using the yScale. Remember that the *y* axis is flipped. A low data value produces a high range value. But even though the range is high, the bar itself should be small. We'll need to re-flip the values just for height so that a low data value produces a small bar and a high data value produces a large bar. To do this, let's subtract whatever the range point is from HEIGHT of the graph. This way, if yScale(datum.count) produces, say, 500, the height of the bar will be 100. We can use yScale(datum.count) normally when adjusting the position of the bars later. Add the following to the bottom of the AJAX callback:

```
d3.selectAll('rect')
    .attr('height', function(datum, index){
        return HEIGHT-yScale(datum.count);
    });
```

Now our rectangles have height, but no width:

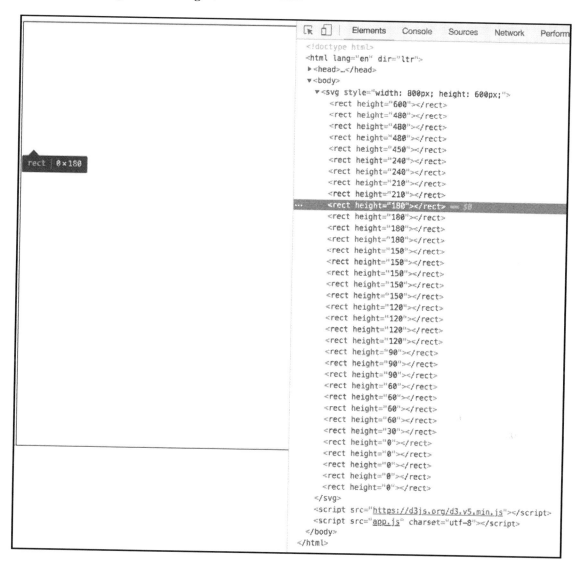

At the bottom of `app.css`, let's give all our bars the same width:

```
rect {
    width: 15px;
}
```

Here's what we should see in Chrome now:

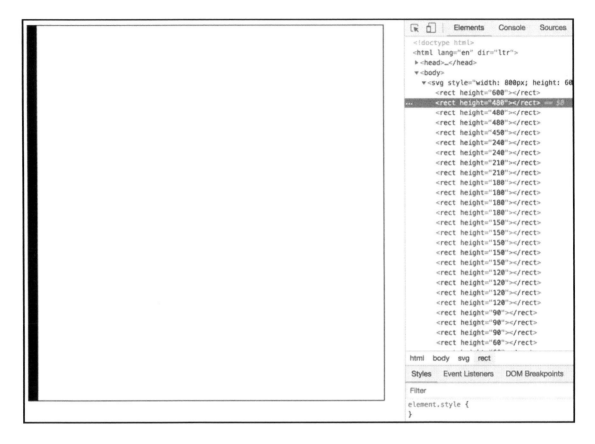

Adjusting the horizontal and the vertical placement of the bars

Our bars all overlap one another at the moment. Let's space them out by mapping x's position to index in the data array. Add the following to the bottom of the AJAX callback:

```
var xScale = d3.scaleLinear(); xScale.range([0, WIDTH]); xScale.domain([0,
data.length]); d3.selectAll('rect') .attr('x', function(datum, index){
return xScale(index); });
```

This maps indices in the array to horizontal range points. Chrome should look as follows:

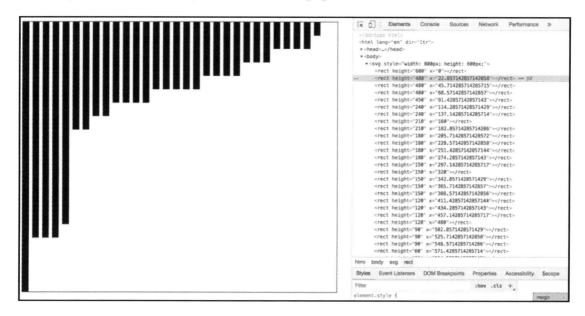

Now let's move the bars so they grow from the bottom, as opposed to hanging from the top. Add the following to the end of the AJAX callback:

```
d3.selectAll('rect')
    .attr('y', function(datum, index){
        return yScale(datum.count);
    });
```

Using our `yScale` function, a high data value produces a low range value, which doesn't push a large bar down much. A low data point produces a high range value, which pushes a small bar down a lot.

Our last few bars don't have any height, because we've mapped the minimum count property of our data to a visual range value of 0 in `yScale`. Let's adjust the last line of this code:

```
var yScale = d3.scaleLinear();
yScale.range([HEIGHT, 0]);
var yMin = d3.min(data, function(datum, index){
    return datum.count;
})
var yMax = d3.max(data, function(datum, index){
    return datum.count;
})
```

```
yScale.domain([yMin, yMax]);
```

We will change it to this code:

```
var yScale = d3.scaleLinear();
yScale.range([HEIGHT, 0]);
var yMin = d3.min(data, function(datum, index){
    return datum.count;
})
var yMax = d3.max(data, function(datum, index){
    return datum.count;
})
yScale.domain([yMin-1, yMax]); //adjust this line
```

Now the domain minimum is one less than what's actually in our data set. Domains with the original minimum are treated as higher values than what's expected for the minimum of the graph. We get this:

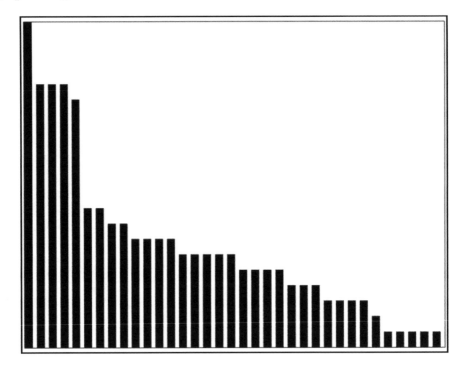

Making the width of the bars dynamic

Currently, our bars have a fixed width. No matter how many elements we have, they have a 15 px width. If we had more data elements, the bars could overlap. Let's change this. Since each `rect` will be the same width, no matter what the data is, we can just assign `width` a computed value. Add the following to the end of the AJAX callback:

```
d3.selectAll('rect')
    .attr('width', WIDTH/data.length);
```

Now let's adjust our `rect` CSS so our bars are more visible:

```
rect {
    /*  remove the width rule that was here */
    stroke:white;
    stroke-width:1px;
}
```

The output will be shown as follows:

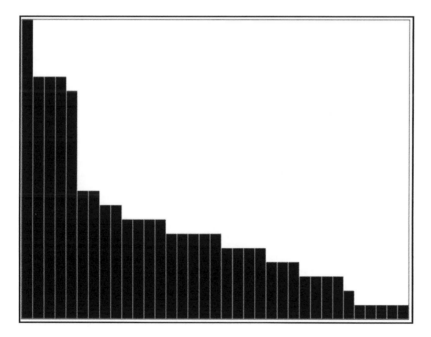

Changing the color of the bar based on data

Right now, the bars are black. A linear scale will interpolate between colors, just like a regular number. Add the following to the end of the AJAX callback:

```
var yDomain = d3.extent(data, function(datum, index){
    return datum.count;
})
var colorScale = d3.scaleLinear();
colorScale.domain(yDomain)
colorScale.range(['#00cc00', 'blue'])
d3.selectAll('rect')
    .attr('fill', function(datum, index){
        return colorScale(datum.count)
    })
```

Notice that we calculate they Domain using d3.extent so that the real minimum of the data set is used to map #00cc00:

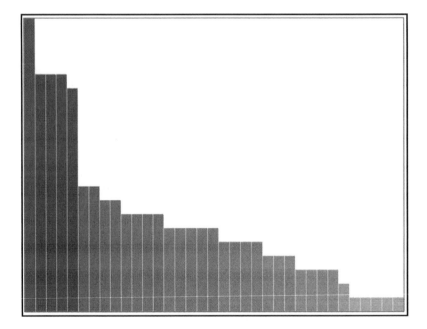

Adding axes

The left axis is the same as shown in `Chapter 4`, *Making a Basic Scatter Plot Interactive*. Add this code to the bottom of the AJAX callback:

```
var leftAxis = d3.axisLeft(yScale);
d3.select('svg')
    .append('g').attr('id', 'left-axis')
    .call(leftAxis);
```

To create the bottom axis, we need to be able to map strings to points on a domain. We'll use a band scale for this, which just divides up the range into equal parts and maps it to an array of discrete values (values that can't be interpolated, for example, strings). Add this code to the bottom of the AJAX callback:

```
var skillScale = d3.scaleBand();
var skillDomain = data.map(function(skill){
    return skill.name
});
skillScale.range([0, WIDTH]);
skillScale.domain(skillDomain);
```

Notice we use `data.map()`. This is regular JavaScript that simply loops through an array and modifies each element based on the given function. It then returns the resulting array, leaving the original array in tact. In the previous example, `skillDomain` will be an array containing the various name properties of each of the data elements.

Once we have an array of each of the skills, we use this as the domain and map each skill to a point within the range. Remember the point in the range is created by dividing up the full range equally based on the number of elements in the domain.

Now that we have a scale that maps each skill text to a point in the *x* range, we can create the bottom axis as before. Add this code to the bottom of the AJAX callback:

```
var bottomAxis = d3.axisBottom(skillScale);
d3.select('svg')
    .append('g').attr('id', 'bottom-axis')
    .call(bottomAxis)
    .attr('transform', 'translate(0,'+HEIGHT+')');
```

We still need to stop the `<svg>` element from clipping the axes. Change the CSS for `svg` in `app.css`:

```
svg {
    overflow: visible;
}
```

The following is the result:

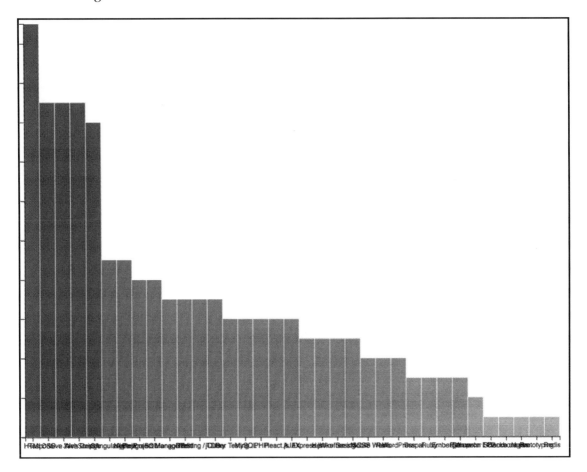

The bottom axis text is all cluttered, though. Let's add some CSS to bottom of `app.css` to fix this:

```
#bottom-axis text {
    transform:rotate(45deg);
}
```

The output will be shown as follows:

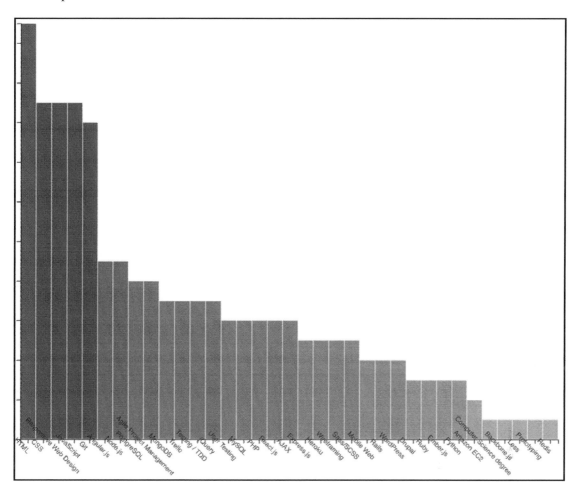

It's rotated, but it's rotated around the center of the element. Let's add a line to what we just wrote, so it rotates around the start of the text:

```
#bottom-axis text {
    transform: rotate(45deg);
    text-anchor: start; /* add this line */
}
```

The output will be shown as follows:

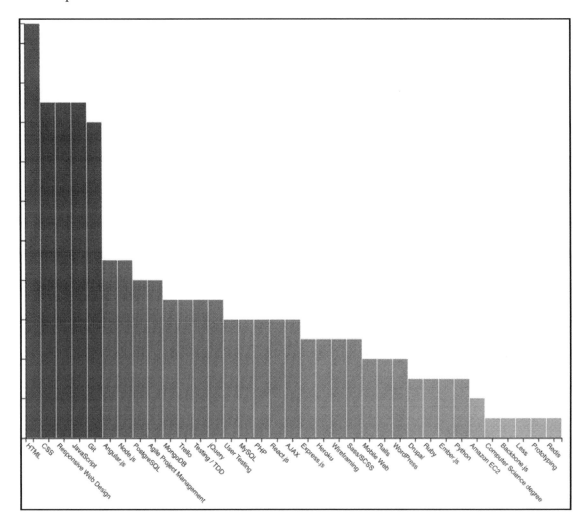

Let's move the graph to the right, so we can see the values for the left axis. Adjust our svg css code so it looks as follows:

```
svg {
    overflow: visible;
    margin-left: 20px; /* add this line */
}
```

Summary

In this chapter, we learned how to use AJAX to make an asynchronous request that will populate a bar graph. In Chapter 6, *Animating SVG Elements to Create an Interactive Pie Chart*, we'll create a pie chart that animates when you remove sections from it.

6
Animating SVG Elements to Create an Interactive Pie Chart

In this chapter, we'll be use animation to make our graphs move. This can give your visualizations a more polished and professional feel.

In this section, we will cover the following topics:

- Creating an ordinal scale
- Creating a color scale
- Adding paths for each pie segment
- Generating an arc creating function
- Formatting the data for the arc
- Adjusting the position of the pie
- Making a donut graph
- Removing parts of the pie

The complete code for this section can be found at `https://github.com/PacktPublishing/D3.js-Quick-Start-Guide/tree/master/Chapter06`.

Setting up the application

As always, we'll need an `index.html` file to house our SVG code. Let's create the file and add the following code to it:

```html
<!DOCTYPE html>
<html>
    <head>
        <meta charset="utf-8">
        <title></title>
        <script src="https://d3js.org/d3.v5.min.js"></script>
    </head>
    <body>
        <svg>
            <g></g>
        </svg>
        <script src="app.js" charset="utf-8"></script>
    </body>
</html>
```

Create data/configuration variables

At the bottom of the `<body>` tag, we're referencing an `app.js` file. Let's create that file and add the following code to it:

```javascript
var WIDTH = 360;
var HEIGHT = 360;
var radius = Math.min(WIDTH, HEIGHT) / 2;

var dataset = [
    { label: 'Bob', count: 10 },
    { label: 'Sally', count: 20 },
    { label: 'Matt', count: 30 },
    { label: 'Jane', count: 40 }
];
console.log(dataset);
```

To be sure that it's working and linked up properly, we've added `console.log(dataset)` to the bottom. Let's open `index.html` in Chrome and view the developer console, to make sure that everything is hooked up the way it should be:

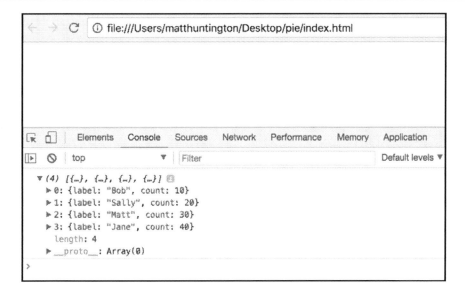

Once we're sure that it's working, we can remove `console.log(dataset);`, as follows:

```
var WIDTH = 360;
var HEIGHT = 360;
var radius = Math.min(WIDTH, HEIGHT) / 2;

var dataset = [
    { label: 'Bob', count: 10 },
    { label: 'Sally', count: 20 },
    { label: 'Matt', count: 30 },
    { label: 'Jane', count: 40 }
];
```

Creating an ordinal scale

An ordinal scale maps a discrete value to some other value. A discrete value is something that can't be divided. Previously, we've used values such as numbers that can be divided up and interpolated. Interpolated just means that for any two numbers, we can find other numbers in between them. For instance, given 10 and 5, we can find values between them (6, 8.2, 7, 9.9, and so on). Now, we want to map values that can't be interpolated—the label properties in our dataset (Bob, Sally, Matt, and Jane). What values lie between Bob and Sally? What about between Bob and Matt? There are none. These are just strings, not numerical values that can be divided up and interpolated.

What we want to do is map these discrete values to other values. The following is an example of how to do this with an ordinal scale. Add the following to the bottom of `app.js`:

```
var mapper = d3.scaleOrdinal();
mapper.range([45, 63, 400]); //list each value for ordinal scales, not just
min/max
mapper.domain(['Bob', 'Sally', 'Zagthor']); //list each value for ordinal
scales, not just min/max

console.log(mapper('Bob'));
console.log(mapper('Sally'));
console.log(mapper('Zagthor'));
```

The previous code should produce the following:

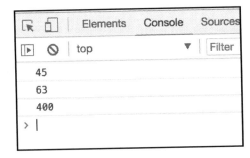

Note that when you are working with ordinal scales, you'll need to list all of the values for both the domain and range. Even if one set is numerical (in the previous case, the range), you'll still have to list each value. If we just listed the min/max for the range, omitting63, D3 would have no idea what value to map Sally to. After all, how close is Sally to Bob,as a value? How close is Sally to Zagth or, as a value? There's no way to calculate that distance, since they're all strings of text, not numbers.

One thing that's surprising is that you can't invert ordinal scales. Remove the previous three `console.log()` statements and temporarily add the following to the bottom of `app.js`:

```
console.log(mapper.invert(45));
```

The following will be displayed:

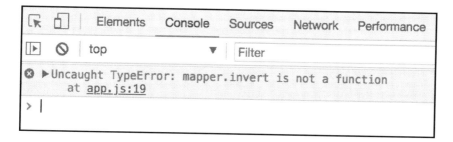

D3 can only go in one direction: from domain to range. You can now remove the `console.log()` statement.

Creating the color scale to map labels to colors

Now, we want to map the label properties of our dataset to colors, instead of random numbers, like in the previous section. We can come up with our own color scheme, or we choose one of D3's sets of colors from `https://github.com/d3/d3-scale-chromatic#categorical`.

If we want to, we can see that these color schemes are just arrays. Temporarily, add the following to the bottom of `app.js`:

```
console.log(d3.schemeCategory10)
```

The following content will be displayed:

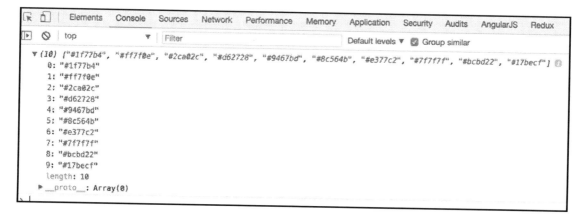

Consequently, we can use a color scheme when setting a range. Replace the previous `console.log()` statement with the following:

```
var colorScale = d3.scaleOrdinal();
colorScale.range(d3.schemeCategory10);
```

We can generate an array of labels for the domain by using JavaScript's native `map` function. Add the following to the bottom of `app.js`:

```
colorScale.domain(dataset.map(function(element){
    return element.label;
}));
```

The following is our code, so far:

```
var WIDTH = 360;
var HEIGHT = 360;
var radius = Math.min(WIDTH, HEIGHT) / 2;

var dataset = [
    { label: 'Bob', count: 10 },
    { label: 'Sally', count: 20 },
    { label: 'Matt', count: 30 },
    { label: 'Jane', count: 40 }
];

var colorScale = d3.scaleOrdinal();
colorScale.range(d3.schemeCategory10);
colorScale.domain(dataset.map(function(element){
    return element.label;
}));
```

Setting up the SVG

The next code block is pretty standard. Add the following code to the bottom of `app.js`:

```
d3.select('svg')
    .attr('width', WIDTH)
    .attr('height', HEIGHT);
```

Adding paths for each pie segment

Let's add path elements for each element in our dataset. Add the following code to the bottom of `app.js`:

```
var path = d3.select('g').selectAll('path')
    .data(dataset)
    .enter()
    .append('path')
    .attr('fill', function(d) {
        return colorScale(d.label);
    });
```

If we examine our elements in the developer tools, we'll see that the paths were added, and each path has a fill value, as determined by `colorScale(d.label)`, which is mapping the label of each data object to a color:

Generating an arc creating function

The paths have fill colors, but no shapes. If you'll recall, the `<path>` elements take a `d=` attribute, which determines how they're drawn. We want to set up something that will somehow map data to a `d=` string, such as the following code (you don't have to add the next code snippet; it's only there for reference):

```
.attr('d', function(datum){
    //return path string here
})
```

Fortunately, D3 can generate the anonymous function that we need for the second parameter of `.attr()` in the previous code snippet. Add the following to `app.js`, just before our previous code for `var path = d3.select('g').selectAll('path')...`:

```
var arc = d3.arc()
    .innerRadius(0) //to make this a donut graph, adjust this value
    .outerRadius(radius);
```

Let's plug this function into its correct place in our previous `var path = d3.select('g').selectAll('path')...` code (it won't work yet, though):

```
var path = d3.select('g').selectAll('path')
    .data(dataset)
    .enter()
    .append('path')
    .attr('d', arc) //add this
    .attr('fill', function(d) {
        return colorScale(d.label);
    });
```

Formatting the data for the arc

The reason that our `arc()` function won't work is the data isn't formatted properly for the function. The arc function that we generated expects the data object to have things like a start angle, an end angle, and so on. Fortunately, D3 can reformat our data so that it will work with our generated `arc()` function. To do this, we'll generate a `pie` function that will take a dataset and add the necessary attributes to it for the start angle, end angle, and so on. Add the following just before the code for `var path =d3.select('g').selectAll('path')...`:

```
var pie = d3.pie()
    .value(function(d) { return d.count; }) //use the 'count' property each
```

```
value in the original array to determine how big the piece of pie should be
    .sort(null); //don't sort the values
```

Our `pie` variable is a function that takes an array of values as a parameter and returns an array of objects that are formatted for our `arc` function. Temporarily add the following code to the bottom of `app.js`, and take a look at the console in Chrome's Developer tools:

```
console.log(pie(dataset));
```

The following content will be displayed:

```
▼ (4) [{…}, {…}, {…}, {…}] ▣
  ▼ 0:
    ▶ data: {label: "Bob", count: 10}
      endAngle: 0.6283185307179586
      index: 0
      padAngle: 0
      startAngle: 0
      value: 10
    ▶ __proto__: Object
  ▼ 1:
    ▶ data: {label: "Sally", count: 20}
      endAngle: 1.8849555921538759
      index: 1
      padAngle: 0
      startAngle: 0.6283185307179586
      value: 20
    ▶ __proto__: Object
  ▼ 2:
    ▶ data: {label: "Matt", count: 30}
      endAngle: 3.7699111843077517
      index: 2
      padAngle: 0
      startAngle: 1.8849555921538759
      value: 30
    ▶ __proto__: Object
  ▼ 3:
    ▶ data: {label: "Jane", count: 40}
      endAngle: 6.283185307179586
      index: 3
      padAngle: 0
      startAngle: 3.7699111843077517
      value: 40
    ▶ __proto__: Object
    length: 4
  ▶ __proto__: Array(0)
```

You can now remove the `console.log(pie(dataset))` call. We can use this `pie()` function when attaching data to our paths. Adjust the previous `var path = d3.select('g').selectAll('path')` code, as follows:

```
var path = d3.select('g').selectAll('path')
    .data(pie(dataset)) //adjust this line to reformat data for arc
    .enter()
    .append('path')
    .attr('d', arc)
    .attr('fill', function(d) {
        return colorScale(d.label);
    });
```

Unfortunately, now, each object from the data array that's been attached to our path elements doesn't have a `.label` property, so our code for `.attr('fill', function(d) {})` is broken. Fortunately, our data does have a `.data` attribute that mirrors what the data looked like before we passed it to the `pie()` function. Let's adjust our `var path = d3.select('g').selectAll('path')` code to use that code, instead, as follows:

```
var path = d3.select('g').selectAll('path')
    .data(pie(dataset))
    .enter()
    .append('path')
    .attr('d', arc)
    .attr('fill', function(d) {
        return colorScale(d.data.label); //use .data property to access
        original data
    });
```

So far, our code is as follows:

```
var WIDTH = 360;
var HEIGHT = 360;
var radius = Math.min(WIDTH, HEIGHT) / 2;

var dataset = [
    { label: 'Bob', count: 10 },
    { label: 'Sally', count: 20 },
    { label: 'Matt', count: 30 },
    { label: 'Jane', count: 40 }
];

var mapper = d3.scaleOrdinal();
var colorScale = d3.scaleOrdinal();
colorScale.range(d3.schemeCategory10);
colorScale.domain(dataset.map(function(element){
    return element.label;
}));

d3.select('svg')
    .attr('width', WIDTH)
    .attr('height', HEIGHT);

var arc = d3.arc()
    .innerRadius(0)
    .outerRadius(radius);

var pie = d3.pie()
    .value(function(d) { return d.count; })
    .sort(null);

var path = d3.select('g').selectAll('path')
    .data(pie(dataset))
    .enter()
    .append('path')
    .attr('d', arc)
    .attr('fill', function(d) {
        return colorScale(d.data.label);
    });
```

The preceding code produces the following result:

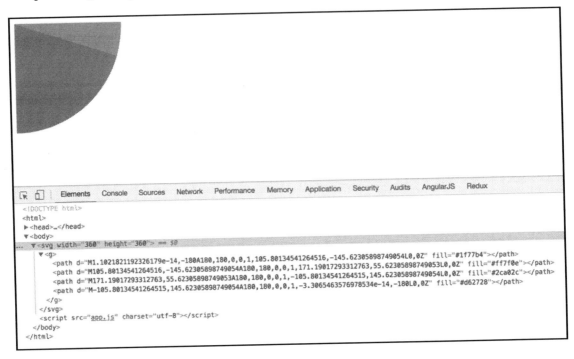

Adjusting the position of the pie

Currently, we can only see the lower-right quarter of the pie graph. This is because the pie starts at $(0, 0)$, but we can move the `group` element containing the pie by adjusting our `d3.select('svg')` code, as follows:

```
d3.select('svg')
    .attr('width', WIDTH)
    .attr('height', HEIGHT);
var container = d3.select('g') //add this line and the next:
    .attr('transform', 'translate(' + (WIDTH / 2) + ',' + (HEIGHT / 2) +
')'); //add this line
```

The pie graph now looks as follows:

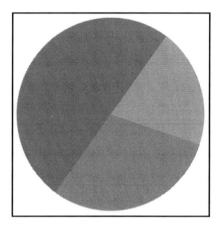

Making a donut graph

If you want the pie to have a hole in the center, just adjust the inner radius of the arc() function, as follows:

```
var arc = d3.arc()
    .innerRadius(100) //to make this a donut graph, adjust this value
    .outerRadius(radius);
```

The graph will now look as follows:

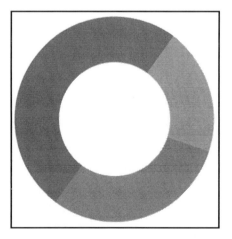

Removing parts of the pie

We want to make it possible to click on a section of the pie to remove it. First, let's add IDs to our data, to make the removal easier. Adjust the `var dataset` code at the top of `app.js`:

```
var dataset = [
    { id: 1, label: 'Bob', count: 10 }, //add id property
    { id: 2, label: 'Sally', count: 20 }, //add id property
    { id: 3, label: 'Matt', count: 30 }, //add id property
    { id: 4, label: 'Jane', count: 40 } //add id property
];
```

Now, let's use those IDs when we map data to paths. Adjust the `.data()` portion of our `var path =d3.select('g').selectAll('path')` code at the bottom of `app.js`, as follows:

```
var path = d3.select('g').selectAll('path')
    .data(pie(dataset), function(datum){ //attach datum.data.id to each
element
        return datum.data.id
    })
```

Let's save a record of the current data for each element by adding a `_current` property to each element (we'll use this later). Add `.each(function(d) { this._current = d; });` to the end of our `var path =d3.select('g')` code, at the bottom of `app.js`:

```
var path = d3.select('g').selectAll('path')
    .data(pie(dataset), function(datum){
        return datum.data.id
    })
    .enter()
    .append('path')
    .attr('d', arc)
    .attr('fill', function(d) {
        return colorScale(d.data.label);
    })//watch out! remove the semicolon here
    .each(function(d) { this._current = d; }); //add this
```

Create the click handler by adding the following code to the bottom of `app.js`:

```
path.on('click', function(clickedDatum, clickedIndex){
});
```

Remove the selected data from the dataset array, using JavaScript's native `filter` function. Adjust the code that we just added, as follows:

```
path.on('click', function(clickedDatum, clickedIndex){
    dataset = dataset.filter(function(currentDatum, currentIndex){ //new
        return clickedDatum.data.id !== currentDatum.id //new
    }); //new
});
```

Remove the `path` elements from the SVG by adding the following to our click handler function:

```
path.on('click', function(clickedDatum, clickedIndex){
    dataset = dataset.filter(function(currentDatum, currentIndex){
        return clickedDatum.data.id !== currentDatum.id
    });
    path //new
        .data(pie(dataset), function(datum){ //new
            return datum.data.id //new
        }) //new
        .exit().remove(); //new
});
```

Now, if we click on the orange segment, we should get the following result:

Let's close the donut and add a transition. Add the following to the bottom of our click handler. Check out the comments in the following code to see what each line does:

```
path.on('click', function(clickedDatum, clickedIndex){
    dataset = dataset.filter(function(currentDatum, currentIndex){
        return clickedDatum.data.id !== currentDatum.id
    });
    path
        .data(pie(dataset), function(datum){
            return datum.data.id
        })
        .exit().remove();

    path.transition() //create the transition
        .duration(750) //add how long the transition takes
        .attrTween('d', function(d) { //tween the d attribute
            var interpolate = d3.interpolate(this._current, d);
            //interpolate
            from what the d attribute was and what it is now
            this._current = interpolate(0); //save new value of data
            return function(t) { //re-run the arc function:
                return arc(interpolate(t));
            };
        });
});
```

Now, when we click on the orange segment, the donut closes smoothly, as follows:

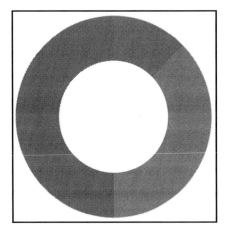

Summary

In this chapter, we created a pie chart that animates when you remove sections from it. You learned how to generate paths from data, so that you can get different parts of the pie without having to specify the drawing commands directly in the path elements. You also learned how to use animation to make visualizations look more professional. Finally, you learned how to remove sections of the pie and have the other path elements redraw themselves, so that the result will be a full pie.

In the next chapter, we will use D3 to create a graph that visualizes the relationships between various nodes of data.

7
Using Physics to Create a Force-Directed Graph

This chapter will cover how to make a force-directed graph that will visualize the relationships between various nodes.

In this lesson, you will learn about the following topics:

- Creating a physics-based force that will center nodes
- Creating a physics-based force that make the nodes repel each other
- Creating a physics-based force that will link the nodes to show their relationships

The complete code for this section can be found at `https://github.com/PacktPublishing/D3.js-Quick-Start-Guide/tree/master/Chapter07`.

What is a force-directed graph?

A **force-directed graph** is a graph that is affected by various forces (such as gravity and repulsion). It can be extremely helpful when creating graphs of relationships.

How to set up a graph of relationships

The following sections will provide an overview of what we're going to build. The overview will cover the display side and the physics side of the implementation.

Display

The display aspect controls what we see; the display will include the following:

- A list of nodes representing people, displayed as circles
- A list of links representing connections between people, displayed as lines

Physics

The physics of the simulation control how the elements interact, as follows:

- A centering force at the center of the SVG will draw all of the nodes toward it
- A repulsive force on each node will prevent the nodes from getting too close to each other
- Link forces will connect each of the nodes, so that they don't repel each other too much

Setting up the HTML

Our file will be a pretty standard `index.html` file, but we'll need two `<g>` elements, as follows:

- One to contain the nodes (**people**: circles)
- One to contain the links (**relationship**: lines)

Here's what our code should look like:

```
<!DOCTYPE html>
<html>
    <head>
        <meta charset="utf-8">
        <title></title>
        <script src="https://d3js.org/d3.v5.min.js"></script>
    </head>
    <body>
        <svg>
            <g id="nodes"></g>
            <g id="links"></g>
        </svg>
        <script src="app.js" charset="utf-8"></script>
    </body>
</html>
```

Setting up styling for nodes and links

Create an `app.css` file for our circles (nodes/people) and lines (links/relationships), as follows:

```css
circle {
    fill: red;
    r: 5;
}

line {
    stroke: grey;
    stroke-width: 1;
}
```

Don't forget to create a link to it in your `index.html` file, as follows:

```html
<head>
    <link rel="stylesheet" href="app.css">
    <script src="https://d3js.org/d3.v5.min.js"></script>
</head>
```

Setting up the SVG

At the top of our `app.js` file, add the following:

```js
var WIDTH = 300;
var HEIGHT = 200;

d3.select("svg")
    .attr("width", WIDTH)
    .attr("height", HEIGHT);
```

If we open `index.html` in Chrome and look at **Elements** in the Developer tools, we should see the following:

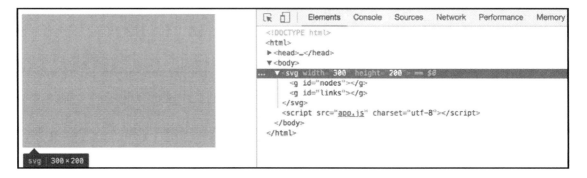

Adding data for people

Let's create an array of people at the bottom of `app.js`, as follows:

```
var nodesData =   [
    {"name": "Charlie"},
    {"name": "Mac"},
    {"name": "Dennis"},
    {"name": "Dee"},
    {"name": "Frank"},
    {"name": "Cricket"}
];
```

Adding data for relationships

Now, let's create the relationships by adding the following array to the bottom of `app.js`. Note that the attributes must be `source` and `target`, in order for D3 to do its magic:

```
var linksData = [
    {"source": "Charlie", "target": "Mac"},
    {"source": "Dennis", "target": "Mac"},
    {"source": "Dennis", "target": "Dee"},
    {"source": "Dee", "target": "Mac"},
    {"source": "Dee", "target": "Frank"},
    {"source": "Cricket", "target": "Dee"}
];
```

Add circles to the SVG

Add the following to the bottom of `app.js`:

```
var nodes = d3.select("#nodes")
    .selectAll("circle")
    .data(nodesData)
    .enter()
    .append("circle");
```

This will create a circle for each element in our `nodesData` array. Our Developer tools should look as follows:

Adding lines to the SVG

Add the following to the bottom of `app.js`:

```
var links = d3.select("#links")
    .selectAll("line")
    .data(linksData)
    .enter()
    .append("line");
```

This will create a line for each element in our `linksData` array. Our Developer tools should look as follows:

Creating a simulation

Now, we'll generate a simulation by adding the following to the bottom of `app.js`:

```
d3.forceSimulation()
```

Note that this simply creates a simulation; it doesn't specify how the simulation should run. Let's tell it which data to act on by modifying the previous line of code, as follows:

```
d3.forceSimulation()
    .nodes(nodesData) // add this line
```

Specifying how the simulation affects visual elements

At this point, our visualization still looks the same, as indicated by the following screenshot:

Let's make our simulation affect the circles/lines that we created, as follows:

- The simulation runs **ticks**, which run very quickly. Think of this a series of steps that happen very quickly, like the ticking of a stopwatch, but faster.
- Each time a new tick occurs, you can update the visual elements. This allows our simulation to animate.
- D3 will calculate and tack positional data onto our regular data, so that we can make use of it.

Add the following to the bottom of `app.js`:

```
d3.forceSimulation()
    .nodes(nodesData)
    .on("tick", function(){
```

```
nodes.attr("cx", function(datum) {return datum.x;})
    .attr("cy", function(datum) {return datum.y;});

links.attr("x1", function(datum) {return datum.source.x;})
    .attr("y1", function(datum) {return datum.source.y;})
    .attr("x2", function(datum) {return datum.target.x;})
    .attr("y2", function(datum) {return datum.target.y;});
});
```

Now, our circles distance themselves from each other a little bit, but this is just a side effect of not having any forces attached to them. We'll add forces next:

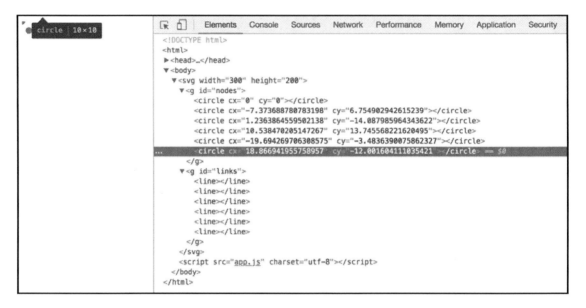

Creating forces

Let's create a centering force at the center of screen, which will pull all of the elements toward it. Adjust the code that we added in the previous step, so that it looks as follows. Not that we only add `.force("center_force", d3.forceCenter(WIDTH / 2, HEIGHT / 2))` to the previous code:

```
d3.forceSimulation()
    .nodes(nodesData)
    // add the line below this comment
    .force("center_force", d3.forceCenter(WIDTH / 2, HEIGHT / 2))
.on("tick", function(){
```

```
nodes.attr("cx", function(datum) {return datum.x;})
    .attr("cy", function(datum) {return datum.y;});

links.attr("x1", function(datum) {return datum.source.x;})
    .attr("y1", function(datum) {return datum.source.y;})
    .attr("x2", function(datum) {return datum.target.x;})
    .attr("y2", function(datum) {return datum.target.y;});
});
```

Now our circles are pulled towards the center of the SVG element:

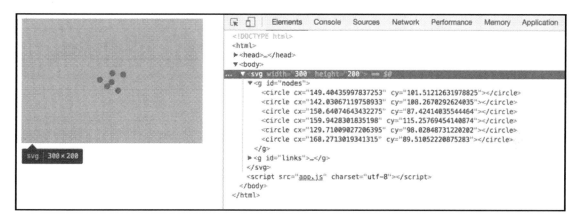

Create a force on each of the nodes, so that they repel each other. Just like in the last step, we will only add `.force("charge_force", d3.forceManyBody())` to the previous code:

```
d3.forceSimulation()
    .nodes(nodesData)
    .force("center_force", d3.forceCenter(WIDTH / 2, HEIGHT / 2))
    // add the line below this comment
    .force("charge_force", d3.forceManyBody())
    .on("tick", function(){
        nodes.attr("cx", function(datum) {return datum.x;})
            .attr("cy", function(datum) {return datum.y;});

        links.attr("x1", function(datum) {return datum.source.x;})
            .attr("y1", function(datum) {return datum.source.y;})
            .attr("x2", function(datum) {return datum.target.x;})
            .attr("y2", function(datum) {return datum.target.y;});
    });
```

You'll notice that the cx/cy values for the circles initially change rapidly, before finally stopping. This is because D3 is running a simulation. Note that center_force is trying to reach a state of equilibrium with charge_force. You'll even notice that when you first load the page, the circles move outward from the center. This is due to the same reason:

Finally, we'll create the links between the nodes, so that they don't repel each other too much. Just like in the last step, we will add the following code to the previous code:

```
.force("links", d3.forceLink(linksData).id(function(datum){
    return datum.name
}).distance(160))
```

Our last chunk of code should now look as follows:

```
d3.forceSimulation()
    .nodes(nodesData)
    .force("center_force", d3.forceCenter(WIDTH / 2, HEIGHT / 2))
    .force("charge_force", d3.forceManyBody())
    //add the three lines below this comment
    .force("links", d3.forceLink(linksData).id(function(datum){
        return datum.name
    }).distance(160))
    .on("tick", function(){
        nodes.attr("cx", function(datum) {return datum.x; })
            .attr("cy", function(datum) {return datum.y; });

        links.attr("x1", function(datum) {return datum.source.x;})
            .attr("y1", function(datum) {return datum.source.y;})
            .attr("x2", function(datum) {return datum.target.x;})
            .attr("y2", function(datum) {return datum.target.y;});
    });
```

- The d3.forceLink function takes the array of links. It then uses the source and target attributes of each link data object to connect the nodes via their `.name` properties (as specified in the return value of the function we just wrote).
- You can tack on `.distance()` to specify how long the lines are visually between each circle.

Finally, our graph looks as follows:

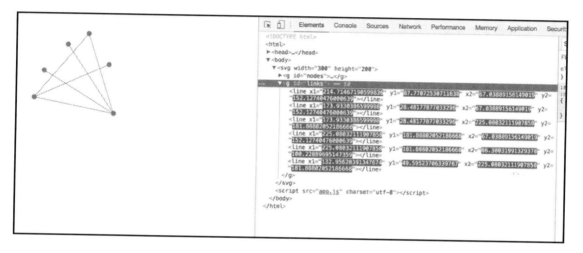

Summary

In this chapter, we used D3 to create a graph that visualizes relationships between various nodes of data. This can be very useful in scenarios such as graphing a friend network, showing parent/child company relationships, or displaying a company's staff hierarchy.

In Chapter 8, *Mapping*, we'll cover how to create a map from GeoJSON data.

8
Mapping

D3 is a great tool for generating maps. To do so, we use specially formatted JSON data to generate `<path>` SVG elements. This specially formatted JSON data is called **GeoJSON**, and in this chapter, we'll use it to create a map of the world.

In this chapter, we will cover the following topics:

- Creating a map
- Defining GeoJSON
- Using a projection
- Generating a `<path>` using a projection and GeoJSON data

The complete code for this chapter can be found at https: `https://github.com/PacktPublishing/D3.js-Quick-Start-Guide/tree/master/Chapter08`.

Defining GeoJSON

GeoJSON is just JSON data that has specific properties that are assigned specific data types. The following is an example of GeoJSON:

```
{
    "type": "Feature",
    "geometry": {
        "type": "Point",
        "coordinates": [125.6, 10.1]
    },
    "properties": {
        "name": "Dinagat Islands"
    }
}
```

In this example, we have one `Feature`, the `geometry` of which is a `Point` with the coordinates [125.6, 10.1]. Its name is `Dinagat Islands`. Each `Feature` will follow this general structure. An example, with the type as `STRING`, is as follows:

```
{
    "type": STRING,
    "geometry": {
        "type": STRING,
        "coordinates": ARRAY
    },
    "properties": OBJECT
}
```

We can also have a `FeatureCollection`, which includes many features grouped together in a `features` array. In the following code snippet, you can see an example of `FeatureCollection` with different `geometry`:

```
{
    "type": "FeatureCollection",
    "features": [
        {
            "type": "Feature",
            "geometry": {
                "type": "Point",
                "coordinates": [102.0, 0.5]
            },
            "properties": {
                "prop0": "value0"
            }
        },
        {
            "type": "Feature",
            "geometry": {
                "type": "LineString",
                "coordinates": [
                    [102.0, 0.0], [103.0, 1.0], [104.0,
                    0.0], [105.0, 1.0]
                ]
            },
            "properties": {
                "prop0": "value0",
                "prop1": 0.0
            }
        },
        {
            "type": "Feature",
            "geometry": {
```

```
            "type": "Polygon",
            "coordinates": [
                [
                    [100.0, 0.0], [101.0, 0.0],
                    [101.0, 1.0], [100.0, 1.0],
                    [100.0, 0.0]
                ]
            ]
        },
        "properties": {
            "prop0": "value0",
            "prop1": { "this": "that" }
        }
    }
]
}
```

Here's the general form:

```
{
    "type": "FeatureCollection",
    "features": ARRAY
}
```

The `features` property is an array of feature objects that were defined previously.

Setting up the HTML

Let's set up a basic D3 page, using the following code:

```
<!DOCTYPE html>
<html lang="en" dir="ltr">
<head>
    <meta charset="utf-8">
    <title></title>
    <script src="https://d3js.org/d3.v5.min.js" charset="utf-8">
    </script>
    <script
src="https://cdn.rawgit.com/mahuntington/mapping-demo/master/map_data3.js"
charset="utf-8">
    </script>
</head>
<body>
```

```
    <svg></svg>
    <script src="app.js" charset="utf-8"></script>
</body>
</html>
```

The only thing different than the setup we've used in previous chapters is the following line:

```
<script
src="https://cdn.rawgit.com/mahuntington/mapping-demo/master/map_data3.js"
charset="utf-8">
</script>
```

The preceding line just loads an external JavaScript file, which sets our GeoJSON data to a variable. The beginning of the code looks as follows:

```
var map_json = {
    type: "FeatureCollection",
    features: [
        {
            type: "Feature",
            id: "AFG",
            properties: {
                name: "Afghanistan"
            },
            geometry: {
                type: "Polygon",
                coordinates: [
                    //lots of coordinates
                ]
            }
        }
        // lots of other countries
    ]
}
```

Note that the `map_json` variable is just a JavaScript object that adheres to the GeoJSON structure (it adds an `idproperty`, which is optional). This is very important. If the object didn't adhere to the GeoJSON structure, D3 would not work as it should.

In production, you would probably make an AJAX call to get this data or, at the very least, create your own GeoJSON file, similar to the one being hosted on `https://rawgit.com/`. The preceding setup was created to make learning easier, by decreasing the complexity associated with AJAX.

Using a projection

Now, let's start on our `app.js` file, as follows:

```
var width = 960;
var height = 490;

d3.select('svg')
    .attr('width', width)
    .attr('height', height);
```

At the bottom of `app.js`, let's add the following code:

```
var worldProjection = d3.geoEquirectangular();
```

This generates a projection, which governs how we're going to display a round world on a flat screen. There are lots of different types of projections that we can use, which can be seen at `https://github.com/d3/d3-geo/blob/master/README.md#azimuthal-projections`.

The preceding line tells D3 to create an `equirectangular` projection (`https://github.com/d3/d3-geo/blob/master/README.md#geoEquirectangular`).

Generating a path using a projection and GeoJSON data

Now that we have our projection, we're going to generate `<path>` elements for each data element in the `map_json.features` array. Then, we will set the fill of each element to `#099`. Add the following to the end of `app.js`:

```
d3.select('svg').selectAll('path')
    .data(map_json.features)
    .enter()
    .append('path')
    .attr('fill', '#099');
```

The following screenshot shows what it should look if we open `index.html` in Chrome and view the **Elements** tab in the Developer tools:

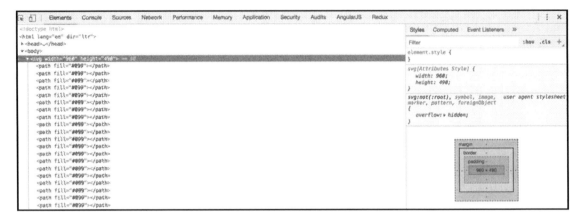

We created the path elements, but they each need a d attribute, which will determine how they will be drawn (that is, their shapes).

We want something like the following:

```
d3.selectAll('path').attr('d', function(datum, index){
    //use datum to generate the value for the 'd' attributes
});
```

Writing the kind of code described in the preceding comment would be very difficult. Luckily, D3 can generate that entire function for us. All we need to do is specify the projection that we created earlier. At the bottom of `app.js`, add the following code:

```
var dAttributeFunction = d3.geoPath()
    .projection(worldProjection);

d3.selectAll('path').attr('d', dAttributeFunction);
```

geoPath() generates the function that we'll use for the d attribute, and the projection (worldProjection) tells it to use the worldProjection variable created earlier, so that the path elements appear as an equirectangular projection, as follows:

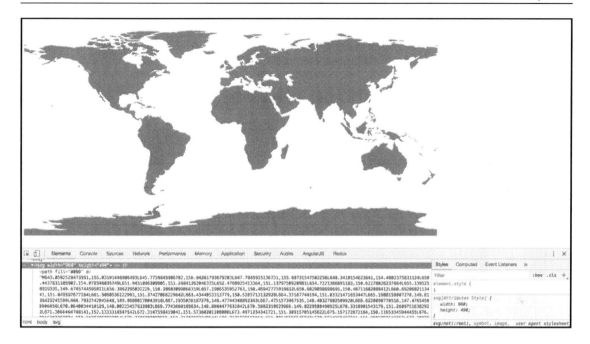

Summary

In this chapter, we discussed GeoJSON, what it's used for, and why it differs from more general JSON data. We've also covered how to use D3 to create a projection and render GeoJSON data as a map. Using this information, we can create all sorts of interesting maps of countries, cities, towns, or any area that we have GeoJSON data for. We can use different projections to view this data in interesting ways

Congratulations! You've made it to the end of the book. Now, go and create amazing visualizations.

Other Books You May Enjoy

If you enjoyed this book, you may be interested in these other books by Packt:

Learning D3.js 5 Mapping – Second Edition
Thomas Newton, Oscar Villarreal, Lars Verspohl

ISBN: 978-1-78728-017-5

- Work with SVG geometric shapes
- Learn to manage map data and plot it with D3.js
- Add interactivity and points of interest to your maps
- Compress and manipulate geoJSON files with the use of topoJSON
- Learn how to write testable D3.js visualizations
- Build a globe with D3.js and Canvas and add interactivity to it
- Create a hexbin map with D3.js

Leave a review - let other readers know what you think

Please share your thoughts on this book with others by leaving a review on the site that you bought it from. If you purchased the book from Amazon, please leave us an honest review on this book's Amazon page. This is vital so that other potential readers can see and use your unbiased opinion to make purchasing decisions, we can understand what our customers think about our products, and our authors can see your feedback on the title that they have worked with Packt to create. It will only take a few minutes of your time, but is valuable to other potential customers, our authors, and Packt. Thank you!

Index